Landscape near Pavia

Aldo Rossi
Architect

A.R. ACADEMY EDITIONS

First published in German in 1993 as the
catalogue for the exhibition Aldo Rossi –
Architekt, 13th March to 2nd May 1993,
Martin-Gropius-Bau, BERLINISCHE GALERIE,
Museum for Modern Art, Photography and
Architecture

Conception and Organisation:
Helmut Geisert (Berlinische Galerie)
Assistants: Ute Raubach
Massimo Scheurer (Studio di architettura
Aldo Rossi, Milan)
Assistant: Maurizio Diton
Translation (English edition): Flora Fischer

English edition published in
Great Britain, 1994 by
ACADEMY EDITIONS
An imprint of Academy Group Ltd

ACADEMY GROUP LTD
Editorial Offices:
42 Leinster Gardens London W2 3AN
Member of the VCH Publishing Group

ISBN 1 85490 364 0

Distributed to the trade in the United States
of America by
ST MARTIN'S PRESS
175 Fifth Avenue New York NY 10010

Printed and bound in Germany

Contents

Berlin
Words of Thanks and a Sardinian Monument

I find this book very beautiful – the blue cover with black writing reminds me of old schoolbooks or collections of fairy-tales. There is something academic, as well as something simple and pedagogical about it.

The exhibition in the Martin-Gropius-Bau also demonstrates the same qualities. It lies at the heart of this city which encompasses such a large portion of European history.

It gives me great pleasure to offer thanks to all my German friends. I thank Isolde and Peter Kottmair, who believe in my architecture but especially in the architecture following the tradition of their city, the beautiful capital of Bavaria. I thank Hans Gerhard Hannesen, with whom I worked on the project for the Museum of German History (*Deutsches Historisches Museum*), for his wonderful essay on my architectural work. In this, armed with great factual knowledge, he combines philosophical exactitude with admiration of my work. I thank Helmut Geisert, who housed the exhibition in 'his' museum. He has enriched this book greatly with his wide-ranging knowledge.

Finally, I am grateful to my Swiss friend Max Scheurer, who accompanied it all and overcame the numerous problems with the stubbornness and precision typical for the Swiss. This stubbornness is both kindly and creative and I appreciate it.

I have thus overcome my natural reservedness or impatience towards making public statements. I still have this, even though a strange fate has often placed me at the centre of arguments, engendered by both hate and love, that I never wished to give the impulse for.

I have not built a great deal in Berlin but I love the two houses in Kochstrasse and Rauchstrasse. Perhaps I was mistaken in following the old tradition of building in Berlin and I do not know how well I actually understood the older city.

I am, however, convinced that cities also grow with 'the idea' people have of them abroad, just as Venice and Florence have become creative elements for travellers and artists, for both German and British culture, since the eighteenth century.

Such was the case with the project for the Museum of German History (*Deutsches Historisches Museum*), which I thought would be constructed. The architects of the National Building Council (*Bundesbaudirektion*) worked on it with eagerness and factual expertise.

These problems do not only apply to our own work: the course of time either destroys or creates situations or feelings that we formerly believed in.

Sometimes I regard time as a plastic object, in which elements whose original meaning we have forgotten, are preserved, alongside the fragments of a beautiful building.

We cannot, however, always put together what has been broken and therefore take little interest in understanding what has been forgotten.

And what of architecture?

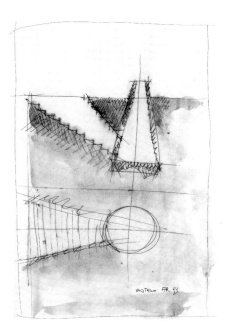

There is a nuraghian monument in Sardinia that I have always attempted both to understand and to imitate. It leads down into the earth and is nothing but a stairway leading to a point, lit from above.

As engineers, we can understand its section to a certain degree if we apply a non-Euclidean geometry, in which the flowing into one another of forms becomes a hidden task.

It always seems to me unbelievable that this great architectural work of art should not belong to the realm of architecture as such. I find it unfortunate that its ancient meaning, if it ever had one, remains a secret.

Aldo Rossi   Milan, February, 1993

Rossi's Berlin

Helmut Geisert

The city of Berlin accompanies Aldo Rossi all the way from his apprentice years, through his years of wandering and on his way towards becoming a citizen of the world. Berlin and Rossi's oeuvre complement one another in many ways, in the magic of invention, for example, linked to the torn, urban character of this wounded city. It not only had to undergo the destruction of war but also had to bear witness to the destruction of whole areas, due to its becoming an ideological parade ground for theories not too well disposed towards the city.

The leading architects of Berlin had prophesied an architecture with a distinctly urban character, fully aware that new architecture had become inextricably linked to the metropolis. This was a result of the nineteenth century, with its great changes in all spheres of life, which greatly influenced the twentieth century, even in its grossly problematic decisions. It includes the dire consequences caused by the rejection of historical monuments, as well as the voluntary acceptance of the uninspiring abstraction of technological progress which one finds in the fetish-like production of industrially fabricated materials, whose appearance can be so deceptive. The most highly developed, industrially produced building material of the nineteenth century was brick. This heralded in programmatically the new manner of building with a hither unknown precision, as, for example, in the form of arches in the interior of Schinkel's Architectural Academy. The architecture of the nineteenth century had actually foreseen everything that has remained of issue in the twentieth century, while rejecting the illusion of being able to invent a completely new style. Rossi works these ideas out anew: he sees the last century as being knowledgeable and self-assured, looks back at it and liberates a formal language that was until then treated more or less canonically. This is also typical for Schinkel. In his designs for suburban churches, he adds either Gothic or Neo-classical facades to the same interiors with supreme ease. The formal articulation thus gains new dimensions. The proportions of the building and therefore its tectonics become a central issue.

'How wonderfully he has combined these elements! How greatly he impresses us with the presence of his work, making us forget that he is simply forcing us to be convinced! There is certainly a divine aspect to these constructions, similar to the forms found by a great writer, who creates a new object from truth and deception in order to delight our limited time on earth.' (JW von Goethe)

This is closely related to an idea of the city, to the customary construction of buildings that could almost be termed naive. Architects were excluded from residential architecture until the end of the last century. The exterior appearance of the streets was influenced by the austere facades of the *Stadtschloss* (Royal Palace) which unconsciously found expression in the proportions of tenement buildings. The idea of the analogous city was therefore always present in Berlin, due to the bourgeois transformation of imperial buildings into residential ones. The question of an architecture that was an expression of the architect's individuality never arose because outward circumstances were not favourable. One has laughed at the naive way of decorating facades according to catalogue designs, chosen randomly by stucco technicians, without taking into account that the tabula rasa offered by the one-dimensional, functional architecture of modernism has brought with it a new poverty rather than a beneficial solution.

In the Sixties, Rossi became interested in Berlin. He was invited as a guest of the Architectural Academy and was familiar with writings on the history of the city. His research came to fruition in sections of the magazine *Casabella Continuità,* of which he has long since been a co-publisher. He has therefore been familiarised for a long time with the issues of the structuring of plots of land, tenement buildings, modern housing estates and the work of Schinkel. During these years of apprenticeship, Rossi attempted to work out the theoretical implications of the concept of the city. This resulted in a book published in 1966, entitled *L'Architettura della Città.*

Characteristically, his initial designs for plots of land in the southern Friedrichstadt express his architectural ideas on the matter he had been concerned with years earlier, namely the tenement building and its incorporation into the urban context, structured into lots and blocks of buildings. In the plans for Kochstrasse, the subdivision of the building reflects the structure of the lots, coming together in a well designed unity. He therefore forges a link with attempts to transform the architectural identity of the tenement building, in the sense of furthering its development. The identity of the tenement building is thus preserved for a spatial programme of changing dimensions.

Even the structure of the business building is derived from the tenement house, an obvious result if one considers the identical structure and utilisation of lots. This becomes visible in the decoration of facades, while the standard height for eaves and the division of storeys remains essentially unchanged. Facades are transformed into street prospects and this is reflected in Rossi's designs. The montage of elements corresponding to one another is an unmistakable characteristic found throughout the project for the Schützenstrasse, while the single houses retain their individuality. The structuring of lots and their changing historical usage puts Rossi's idea of the analogous city to the test and it becomes wonderfully self-evident. Another successful attempt was the former Stalinallee (later Karl-Marx-Allee, now Frankfurter Allee). Here, one tried to construct a metropolitan street against the background of a tenement city in ruins, referring to urbanistic forms and dimensions reminiscent of 1900. Rossi feels sympathy for this project and refers to it affectionately in his design for the Landsberger Allee.

11

Knowing the transitory character of the nineteenth century, Rossi's architecture gains a programmatic character for a city that stems largely from this period. The transformation of historical forms into unexpected, new creations, appearing to arise from a child-like world of dreams, is appropriate for the bourgeois age.

This spectral quality can also be found in drawings by Friedrich Gilly and is surely linked to experiencing the stillness of timelessness, diametrically opposed to a continuity of a history of styles that brings with it nothing but fashionable trends unsuitable for historical cities.

One could ask oneself how Schinkel would have developed 'in Ambrosian manner' and if the rather playful architecture described by Theodor Hetzer would have undergone a new synthesis. This has become an issue in Rossi's enlivening designs for Berlin. He holds a mirror up to the city so that it can become more aware of itself, due to his recognition of its formal language. 'The recognition of cities is linked to the decoding of their images uttered in dreams' (S Kracauer) – this recognition, integrated into the planning, appears to hold up a mirror in which dream and reality melt into one another, as in Romanticism, the origin of modern city planning, where previously unknown worlds, also horrific ones, remain forever alive in our imaginations.

The interest now taken in Aldo Rossi's work stems from the goals of important architectural developments of the late nineteenth century and includes a critique of subsequent developments, particularly those created by the simpler minds of the functionalists. This is all the more appropriate in a city inextricably linked to these historical developments. The development of architecture has been closely connected to urban life since the Renaissance. This was also the case in *Gründerzeit* Berlin, where the cityscape changed within a few years, swallowing up surrounding areas. It remains an irony of history that developments brought about by the city were confused with urban development. The estates of the Twenties, these wonderful modernist projects, have had a major influence on the dissolution of the city. These *petits bourgeois* living experiments have stabbed the city in the back. Today, one should attempt a new idea of the metropolis, in order to stem the increasing course of its dissolution. This is the central idea behind Rossi's new project for Berlin, that would like to evolve into a poetics of the city. It succeeds because the memories of the inhabitants recognise forms, figures, surfaces and colours that have been made contemporary but appear like childhood memories. Houses are made individual when their inhabitants use them, in order to write their own history. This can only be a happy one if it gains shared traits – children's games in a metropolis are possible only in architecture that creates protected courtyards. This places clear limits in architectural invention.

'The parties are soon over while the palaces remain! People and not houses are unlucky!' (Albert Ehrenstein)

Introduction

Alberto Ferlenga

In the case of Aldo Rossi, the image always precedes and accompanies the architect's work.

In his oil paintings, woodcuts, ink drawings or lithographs, the characters of urban scenes act out the gestures, tones and situations with which they want to, or have to, be confronted with. They encounter the shadows of memory and history, measure themselves against these, cross the cities and take the objects of everyday life up into their expressions.

Confrontations, parallels and fragments are the main characteristics of these works of art. They seem to fulfil the task that Bernini ascribed to a deforming, magnifying glass, which he took on his journey through France. He recommended its use to all artists. Did it not offer the opportunity, in his opinion, of transforming colours and dimensions? It distorts the way one perceives designs, takes them out of the habitual and allows the architect to judge his work and get to know his own nature from an unusual point of view, armed with the requisite disinterestedness. In his paintings, that have a parallel life with his designs in a certain sense, Rossi tries to find new approaches and to depict things scenically. He creates analogies, and therefore liberates the architect from the shackles created by the original context. Fragments of well known designs are found in countless variations in his pictures. These can either serve as inspiration for further designs or content themselves with a nostalgic journey back to a possible form of existence.

At the same time, a unique 'destructive vein' seems to run through this body of work. The broken lines of Gallaratese and other buildings rise up from a modern landscape of ruins in a famous print made in 1974, entitled 'Murdered Architecture'. It is as if Rossi is searching for a closer relationship to the breakdown of the cities, by formally inverting pictures from his personal repertoire. In other pictures he combines buildings with objects or figures from an 'architectural bestiary'. The scale changes, objects are dissolved into single elements, architecture seems dominated by a process of contortion in which it constantly shifts and reveals hidden aspects.

The succession of narrative writings constantly surpasses our expectations. These have the crazy and prophetic structure of a novel by Malcolm Lowry. They also evoke paintings by Sironi in which forms dissolve into almost abstract quotations, cities lose their identity. The frame itself, however, remains and further depictions forge their way ahead.

Some pictures obviously wish to preserve the fate of the buildings forever. Rossi likes to recall the similarity between the initial sketch and the finished building as being characteristic of his manner of working. The more time that passes, the stronger the similarity seems to become, as in the designs for the buildings in Turin and Fukuoka – it appears able to foresee, rather than exclude, possible developments within the process of building and possible, new 'infections'. It tries to leave behind a strong impression, or knows it will last forever, far removed from changes that the wear and tear of time brings with it.

The 'homely', personal pictures reveal yet another universe. They are much more literary in character. Rossi reveals the characteristic and paradoxical 'disinterest in architecture' which he likes to lay claim to in a highly concrete manner.

The Milanese or American interiors, the horses and dogs of several recent pictures, are reflexes of an interior geography, for which architecture forms but the background seen from a distance, framed by a window or with the arrangement of certain objects. One could come to believe that these set up the prerequisites for architecture. What they actually do is to reveal the circumstances under which it is created, its autobiographical traits. At the same time, these interiors indicate an interior mystification of place, the process of the liberation of topoi, the transformation of simple forms, revealing a key to an interpretation of the poetics and architecture of Aldo Rossi.

A Conversation

Aldo Rossi and Bernard Huet

B. Huet: For a while, one had only heard of Aldo Rossi as a theoretician and author of the famous book *The Architecture of the City*. Quite soon, however, the poetic world of Aldo Rossi was discovered quite far removed from a conventional approach to architecture, in wonderful architectural designs and strongly autobiographical pictures. Then, one day, came the realisation that Aldo Rossi not only designs theoretical projects but actually constructs them.

These three areas, where you have been almost equally active at a certain point in your life, in my opinion, represent the three inextricably related and complementary aspects of your contribution to the architecture of the second half of the twentieth century.

I should very much like to know how you dedicate your time to these three activities and what importance they have in the creation of your work – especially in an age in which one encounters the utterly 'one-sided' type of professional architect (who some would call manager-architect).

A. Rossi: I believe that every artist, scientist and researcher's life has the potential of encompassing constantly diverging and highly differing activities, existing alongside each other. Sometimes, at a given moment, one of these activities dominates the others. Therefore, the writer Aldo Rossi, the painter Aldo Rossi and the architect Aldo Rossi are non-existent. I simply regard these various aspects as a unity (as do all artists, in my opinion) and I therefore particularly enjoy opportunities where I can express myself as technician, artist and writer. At certain moments in my life a number of circumstances have come together that one could compare to Baudelaire's concept of 'correspondences'. These relationships between people, the interrelation of historical and personal experience, are important in order to understand the reasons for preferring one activity to another.

When I started to concentrate on architecture, writing, for example, played an important role. My education was basically a literary one and I therefore regarded writing as an essential path towards liberation from the catastrophic state of architecture in the Sixties, when I completed my studies at the polytechnic. It appeared important to work out a theoretical basis and not to completely divorce oneself from the historical aspect of modernism. One should, however, divorce oneself from professional architecture (for me, this includes both that in Milan, as well as that encountered in the rest of Europe) that was based on modernism and had rejected all theoretical concepts of architecture.

My love of literature and my intention to deepen my relatively lesser interest in architecture on a theoretical basis spurred me on to write the essays in *Casabella Continuità* and later the books with which you are familiar. They have made me well known both in France and all over the world.

I must add that I never felt that I was particularly destined to become an architect and as we were just speaking of circumstances where I might have become, shall we say, a soldier or an actor, then I should have probably been able to work just as efficiently. I did not make a clear decision to become an architect. I could have as easily studied medicine as architecture.

After completing my studies, while working as an architect, I spent much more time on architecture than on other subjects. Even today, however, while writing a text in memory of a recently deceased friend, I experience greater pleasure in writing and speaking than during my work as an architect.

Without wishing to put myself in the category of great artists, I believe that it is a characteristic of the human spirit to want to expand within the area it has dedicated itself to. If Picasso had been a writer, he would have been a great one, just as Dante would have been a great painter, had he painted. A particular profession does not call for the brain to have a particular characteristic. It is rather that working in a particular profession develops the area in question, even if the spirit is ill prepared for it.

B.Huet: One could assume that you now dedicate yourself completely to the completion of numerous projects all over the world and I do not know if you have enough time and opportunity to develop new theoretical ideas.

There was a time when the abstract qualities of projects that remained in the planning stage or were sometimes, as at Gallaratese, constructed, gave these an exemplary, demonstrative value. This appears not to be the case any longer today. Your mature architecture has gained greater depth in terms of scale and material, that has made it more subjective (in this I see an application of the famous slogan, 'analogous' architecture that you referred to at the end of the Seventies), so that they could at least seem to appear pragmatic. And yet, every time I see a new design of yours, I am surprised to note how greatly your architecture is influenced by an implicit use of the theory, that I should like to work out clearly sometime. Could you perhaps explain how your present projects link up with the continuity of theoretical ideas that you formulated more than twenty years ago?

A.Rossi: I believe that I have created basic architectural principles that can be fairly easily designed and built, both for myself and my co-workers. Alongside of this, I teach and have also brought the knowledge of these theoretical basics to a great number of young architects.

16

I am only superficially annoyed by the frequent accusation that there is a young architectural movement that imitates me and builds like Rossi all over the world. In actual fact, this does not disturb me. I should even go so far as to say that it makes me contented, for I have essentially achieved what I wanted. I am convinced that one can develop one's own personality only after one has learnt precise basics in architecture. It is the same with a language – if one does not master the basics, if one does not learn the basic rules of the French language, one cannot speak it. Of all those speaking French, there will be a few geniuses like Racine but these will be few and far between. Anyone can develop an individualistic style if they start out by using the language itself. Similarly, if one points out so-called imitations of my work in Japan or Latin America, I see it in a different light. It seems to me that every architect develops his own special qualities and that these could perhaps be better than mine in their own way.

Let us take an example that means much to me. Palladio, as we know, created a style of architecture that is closely linked to the spirit of a place, to the 'genius loci'. Therefore, one finds the Venetian Palladio of villas and palaces, as well as the Palladio visible throughout the world – from Louisiana to Russia, from England to France – where a wonderful form of Palladian architecture has developed. I believe that certain English Palladian architects, such as the Adams brothers, have sometimes reached greater perfection than Palladio himself. They raised Palladian architecture to its peak, and yet there is still a difference between this perfection and the Palladio in Vicenza, or the Palladianism of his Italian imitators who tend to be much more Baroque. I cite this example to show that the basic principles of an architectural style, once they have been created, exist over long periods of time and are capable of development. Modernism has already partially attempted to do this, although I believe that its notorious failures result from the fact that it created a caesura, not something continuous.

B.Huet: I find that what you are saying is highly important for an understanding of your work on the language of architecture. What strikes one immediately about your work is its substantiality, its coherence and continuity. You have defended this against rain and storm without making concessions to fashion.

In an age in which difficulty and long-windedness are often regarded as virtues, your architecture draws strength and truth from its direct language and unmistakable style. This simplicity, however, creates a complex manner of perception in the viewer. Faced by your designs or buildings, one is often overcome by a strange feeling, a mixture of familiarity with something already seen and recognised, and the alienating effect of a rather strange poetic vision.

The basic elements of your language are a small number of terms, syntagmas and topoi. You vary, decline and shift their meaning sensitively, take them up again and repeat them. This relates your manner of thinking to that of a number of contemporary artists. It would appear that it would be easy to catalogue the number of Aldo Rossi's inventions. The reality of the situation is, however, much more complex.

Apart from the problems relating to language, there are two aspects of your work that I should like to discuss with you. The first arises from the question of typology. You have said that your architecture draws from certainties that arise both from the archetypes of erudite architecture and from typology in the classical sense of the word. Apart from this, one can see from the poetry found in your stock of pictures that you draw substance from everyday objects (chimney factories, bathing cabins on the Island of Elba, the coffee machine etc). Taking this into account, within the limits set by any comparison, it is perhaps not incorrect to relate your manner of thinking to that of Robert Venturi. If one imagines to what degree everyday objects originate in a highly typological universe, one can see how completely typology and poetry, in your opinion, are unified.

Numerous contemporary architects reject any concessions to typology under the flagship of artistic freedom. They believed this to be too strict to allow them to combine it with the expression of their individual creativity. How do you deal with what appears to be highly contradictory?

A. Rossi: If an architect states that typology is too strict, he is simply demonstrating his ignorance and stupidity. Typology is a technical term that has always been used in architecture to define certain types of buildings and styles of building. In the course of centuries, the typology of the palace has become fixed. The palaces of the Renaissance were constructed according to this typology and yet Renaissance architecture is extraordinarily diverse. Milizia described architects incapable of finishing a building in the following manner: 'They have failed to grasp the general idea of the building'. He is referring to typology in this case.

This debate seems based on a minor and irrelevant misunderstanding. If I am supposed to build a room, I have to know how large it should be, if it should have right angles or be square and if it should, or should not, lead onto a corridor. There are a number of specific relationships that the architect must take into account and these exist in all areas of life. I am not a rider but I believe that one can distinguish between several schools of riding – the American, Italian, French etc. This in no way lessens the worth of horse or rider.

Observing even the most everyday of phenomena is hugely important for me. I always tell my co-workers and students that they should, above all, look at things because it is through observation that one can learn the most.

Someone visiting Paris can, for example, go to a museum or simply go for a walk, and this view of the city can be enough to enrich his individual style of architecture. An observation is related to a design in a certain manner, and I believe that this answers the question you asked about how one can build various houses in Japan, the United States, Germany and elsewhere, starting out from one basic position. The results gained from observation actually always visibly enrich a project.

Let us take the important insights I gained during the construction of the hotel 'Il Palazzo' in Fukuoka, in Japan, as an example. A dialectic relationship soon developed between the Japanese architects, who greatly admired my work and who would have liked me to be a little more like Aldo Rossi for this project, and myself, wanting to be a little Japanese, as the result of observation, rather than from a preconceived idea. Many typically Japanese objects that I observed around me and liked naturally found an echo in my designs. This always occurs when there is a mutual exchange of interests. To return to the question – this is rather similar to the farmhouses in Louisiana (that you are perhaps more familiar with than I), that one recognises because of their typology and their porches with columns, above all because one is familiar with Palladio, even if these Palladian houses have little in common with Palladio.

B. Huet: Your answer has, however, failed to deal with the problem of invention. You know a generation of architects, who a certain specialist press has spurred on to consider their work as the 'new' architecture of modernism, without recognising exactly on what they base this and which modernity we are actually speaking of. What role does invention play in your architectural oeuvre?

A. Rossi: Invention is a way of life for me and should never be made problematic. I cannot, and will not, make demands on myself to invent a new architecture. I create architecture and express certain things by doing so. I have, however, never forced myself to invent something and I shall never do so. Anyone can invent something if they are able to express their own individuality.

B. Huet: I understand your answer as an expression of your basic point of view. I believe, however, that despite this, one can detect architectural spaces and ensembles that could be termed inventions, by looking closely at certain projects. I should like to cite the example of the cylindrical room that runs through the whole height of a project and receives light from the top, as one can see in the design for the Congress Palace in Milan. This was also constructed in the form of a lobby in the theatre in Genoa. Is it not possible to regard this unique room as one of Aldo Rossi's inventions?

A. Rossi: No, because for me this results from observation. Hundreds upon thousands of people could see exactly the same thing, while each individual has a different view of it. It is rather like falling in love: one meets many people and nothing happens and then one falls in love with a specific individual. I have been interested in the idea of the 'sky light', the light falling from heaven, for a long time and have mentioned it often in my lectures. I remember that the large, glass-covered inner courtyard, above all the one at the University of Zurich, impressed me greatly. When I was on a lecture tour in Columbia some time ago I went to see a tourist attraction, the Cathedral of Christ. The Spanish conquerors fortified and extended former mines, left empty by the Indios. They used the light falling from above and placed a large, wooden Christ against a wall in such a manner that it would be lit up by the rays of the rising and setting sun. Thousands have seen this installation. It impressed me greatly because here the architecture reached the sublime, so that one can no longer speak of the categories of architecture, nature or religion. I do not know which particular major or soldier of the conquering army had the idea of putting the light of the mine to such a use, but he certainly succeeded in creating great architecture. The idea of the 'sky light' is therefore not my own invention but arises from an observation and is of great importance in my buildings. I probably had the idea of light falling from above before I ever went to Columbia. The chapel in the cemetery in Giussano consists solely of light in its upper regions, as if death came from heaven and not from earth.

B. Huet: If I understand you correctly, you are saying that nothing can be really new for you. There is therefore no need to invent anew, as it is sufficient to make precise observations and then to describe this in an innovative manner. This manner of re-transcribing, however, is not as obvious as it may appear.

A. Rossi: It is certainly not all that simple!

B. Huet: It is not simple! This indicates the root of the problem.

I should like to turn to a question that is closely linked to the continuity and uniformity of your style. Your critics often accuse you of being insensitive to context and of constantly producing the same architecture, whether it be in Milan, Berlin, Tokyo or Paris. I cannot accept such criticisms that obviously indicate lack of knowledge about your buildings. I see the issue in a different light. One sees one of these constructions and cannot help immediately thinking that it is by Rossi, which I find quite normal. If one decides, however, to compare various buildings, one does become aware of contextual differences. This applies to the impression created by the whole, to certain details, such as special materials only specific to a certain place, or even certain unexpected, architecturally theatrical effects. Which role do your reactions to the Parisian context play in relation to the council apartments that you built there?

A. Rossi: Let us say that the inspiration I had in Paris was rather banal. I read in some magazine that I had built like Haussmann once again, that I had rebuilt the roofs of Paris. This is true and I do not find the remark in the least insulting. I just do not understand why the roof that I constructed in La Villette should not be a Paris roof in the original sense, at the same time as being something modern and new. This roof, inextricably linked to the idea we have of Paris, particularly of the Rue de Rivoli, pointing upwards in a way as to almost form an individual metallic building, could have taken an entirely different form. Determined by local form, it is recognisable by any tourist. It is an integral element of Parisian architecture and became the dominant element of my design. I believe that this building will have a far greater effect on the city than the buildings of the avant-garde, which had little relationship to the physical reality of Paris. I was recently asked to go to Bordeaux for a project and I heard the same kind of criticism there. Despite my love for France, I must say that I have never had a great deal of luck in this country and I have built hardly anything here. I have been asked several times, without being made any concrete offers. Therefore, my experiences in France have been minor ones. At the moment, I am working on the small museum at Vassivière, which I owe to one of my former students, a Frenchman who lives in Switzerland.

B. Huet: But La Villette is a rather important project.

A. Rossi: That is correct. I did not wish to complain. Let us just say that I did not have the same kinds of experiences in France as I did in Germany, Japan or other countries. I think that the French do not really like my architecture!

B. Huet: This impression can be reversed.

I should now like to turn to the relationship between the design and the constructed project. You belong to the party that speaks of the design as absolutely central in architecture, but this must be followed by a transition to the construction of a building. In the work of many architects one finds that this transition leads to a loss of substance. Sometimes an inefficiently realised project changes the design until it becomes unrecognisable. At other times, as is often the case nowadays, the construction looks like the mechanical or abstract enlargement of the model or design. If one studies the history of these designs, one discovers several that were realised with hardly any changes. On the other hand, there are models that were visibly changed for economical, technical or functional reasons. Taking the house in La Villette as an example, one can see that the project went through a number of changes from the initial competition design to the finished building. The history of these changes would perhaps be of interest for an understanding of the changes acceptable, or unacceptable, to the architect. To put it another way, one could discover from this what you regard as essential and what you find of lesser importance in architecture. Each project has its own history and this is part of the history of all the projects.

A. Rossi: Let us differentiate between two things. First, I agree with what you have just said about the history of all the projects. It is correct that history is also a part of a project. Importantly, large projects such as The Louvre or The Dome of St Peter's all have a long history, like an architectural treatise. I am naturally interested in this, even though I did not build The Louvre or St Peter's myself. The minor building has a similar history, not only of a technical nature; the succession of various overlords, law-makers, owners and epochs is a part of this. Let us take the example of the town hall of Borgoricco, that was realised according to the model, despite everything. This small Venetian city has seen so many changes – a succession of municipal councils and administrations, each demanding one thing and then asking for its exact opposite – and all this in the end contributes to the history of a building, which is as it should be.

In regard to the relationship between the design and the constructed building, I believe, and am proud of the fact, that in most cases this has almost been perfect. If one looks at the Casa Aurora, the headquarters of GFT in Turin, one observes that the photographs of the finished building are identical with the initial design sketches. This is the same with the town hall at Borgoricco or with my latest projects constructed in the USA. The architecture has remained unchanged, yet there may have been improvements of a technical nature, although resulting from other deliberations. Today's architect must become more and more of a technician. He has to increase his understanding of problems all the time. I believe that I have achieved a certain maturity in this sphere. Architecture is increasingly becoming a collective undertaking. This makes it advantageous to work with technicians specialised for each part of the construction. At the same time, I do not need to give up my own role. At the moment, I am preparing the design drawings for the Congress Palace in Milan. I have attempted to create and define a structural type for the roof covering (highly important because of its scale). I could then work with the engineers who can modify and correct the structure. I do not believe that the architect can have control over everything except in the sense that he must be capable of imagining and discussing what is feasible. It would certainly be absurd to reject the high quality of today's technology.

B.Huet: Nonetheless, I have a more individual explanation for your manner of working. It is a mistake to accuse you of designing projects in Milan, sending them abroad and not worrying too much about their construction, as the finished building ostensibly carries your stamp. There is, however, one thing that I find hard to comprehend. Sometimes, projects have come into conflict with a construction that contradicts the basic idea of the design. I have already mentioned this in the case of La Villette in Paris but it also applies to the Friedrichstrasse in Berlin. The typology of the council apartment 'with pergolas' that you favour is unacceptable in both Berlin and Paris. It is surprising to discover your ability to accept typological changes, while still keeping to the architectural idea of the design. In the same way, you seem to pay little attention to the sketched detail during the construction phase (which does not mean that you consider detail as being unimportant), in order to deal with scale and exact proportion highly generously. In this, you act very different to the widely practised manner of the 'artistic architects' who demand a manic control over the building. They appear to believe that detail is the architect's signature. One could certainly say that this tendency is even more paradoxical because today's architecture makes a sharing of the work during construction, interdisciplinary teams and the use of industrially mass produced products (steel, metal casing, etc) unavoidable. What is admirable about your work is that it is based on a realistic assessment of these forms of production. Your projects demonstrate such elementary, essential architectural qualities that the idea and the poetry of the design cannot be altered by concessions made towards a certain system of construction and the details of its completion. Does this sum up your ideas about the construction phase?

A. Rossi: Yes, indeed it does.

B. Huet: I could, by the way, cite many examples from the history of architecture that demonstrate similarities to your work. Several significant creations by Michelangelo were completed after his death, following more or less precise handwritten instructions. The poetry of the artist is so powerful that the details can be liberated from authenticity.

A. Rossi: In my opinion, you have just answered the question yourself, although there is something I should like to add. First of all, I believe that what you said about serial production is of basic importance for the architect. I believe that I am a truly contemporary architect because I use modern technology in the way that it should be used. While I was studying at the polytechnic in Milan, we were told to draw single parts of metal casing – I do not think students nowadays do this anymore. I remember that I even failed several times because it is a difficult task – the system has to be closed off in an air-tight manner, has to work efficiently etc. I actually think that this is a mistake, do you not agree? I always refused to do this as there are a number of specialised companies where technicians and engineers spend their lives conceiving and producing metal casing. I shall not name any names, as this would be a form of advertisement, but is it not ridiculous for a contemporary architect to spend time drawing metal casing? As if one could study the valve of a Mercedes engine! The designer creates the parts and they are bought when needed! I therefore believe that I have an ultra-modern attitude to this problem. Architects who concern themselves with the technology of laying tiles, or that of metal casing, seem to me to be archaic. If an architect feels the need to be in control of every centimetre of his project he must surely be rather limited and cannot have a very generous attitude towards his own architecture.

In order to answer your question, it would suffice to remember Alberti, who perhaps never saw a building of his after it had been constructed, or Michelangelo, who gave instructions regarding the approximate height of the columns of the Laurentian Library in letters sent to Florence. In the wonderful collection of Palladio's designs, which I was able to see, thanks to the generosity of the Royal Institute of British Architects, one realises that he also did not draw details. He limited himself to sketches or indicated several other projects that had already been completed and which demonstrated clearly the spirit of the building he wished to create. A building such as the Casa Aurora, for example, will not be altered if one shortens the columns by two centimetres.

I therefore regard the construction phase with a certain degree of easiness. Although I would deny that I simply sent off a design to Japan, I followed the progress of the project in Fukuoka, for example, most carefully. What does it in fact mean to 'follow the progress of a project'? If one wants to have bricks or supports that are produced in a certain manner, one has to know exactly what one is looking for. As I had absolutely no idea how the Japanese produce bricks I checked two or three samples and then chose a type that is actually of better quality than bricks fired in Lombardy.

B. *Huet:* I was actually just about to ask you about your relationship to systems of construction. You have always defended yourself in this sphere, by pointing out that you studied at the polytechnic in Milan and therefore regard yourself as an engineer. I believe that such an answer is biographically correct, but it fails to explain the significance of systems of construction in the way you perceive architecture. I dare to set up the hypothesis that the concessions you make towards systems of construction are purely typological, apart from unusual buildings such as the Congress Palace in Milan, which you have referred to. Systems of construction represent for you an ensemble of conventions and topoi inextricably linked to the system of architectural forms. Carrying walls, rafters, columns and attics are integral elements of your language and therefore have no independent identity in the construction. To my mind, this conception is in strong contradiction to a tendency (very much the case in France at present) that favours revealing of structures and constructive decoration as expressions of architectural modernity. How do you see this trend?

A. *Rossi:* First of all, I do not believe that the essential aims of architecture can be achieved by these means. Technological developments increasingly lead to simplicity in structure, as well as increasing clarity of decision. If one makes structures and techniques visible, one is always limited by the times and is often already outdated, regarding the future. Let us take an example that we are familiar with, as we sadly spend a great deal of time in airports, as do all contemporary architects. Let us compare two great European airports: Paris and Frankfurt. I do

24

not know how old Roissy is – perhaps ten years old? Whatever the case may be, one wanted to look to the future and furnished it in a truly immaculate manner. It is a 'body building' made of structures, sluice gates and lifts. When one arrived at this large Parisian airport at the time when it was built, one felt as if one was entering the future. Perhaps ten years have passed, and honestly, with all due respect to French technology, the airport 'works badly', is ugly and outdated. Frankfurt Airport is particularly simple – no ostentation, utterly ordinary structures – and although it was built during the same period, it is a modern airport that 'works'. By saying this I wish to point out that technology must always be within the realms of feasibility and does not need to appertain to a fake future.

It is the Futurist Marinetti's old idea that Milan must be a truly modern city, as it resounds with the 'noise of trams'. Today, this image of the noise of trams on their tracks reminds us of the past. There is nothing worse than foreseeing the future. It is the fate of all science fiction to theatrically reveal simplified and rapidly outdated structures.

B. *Huet:* I have just realised that in defending the building at La Villette you unconsciously used the same arguments one has observed in Adolf Loos' reply to criticisms of the famous building on Michaelerplatz in Vienna. Do you remember what he wrote? I will quote him (not exactly): 'I did not wish to make this building into an avant-garde manifesto, but just simply build a house, as did the old masters.' Loos' modernity is based on a wish to continue authentic, forgotten traditions.

Is it actually true that in an answer to a journalist's question asking whether you are modern or postmodern, you replied: 'No, I cannot be postmodern, as I have never even been modern.' How would you describe your present attitude towards modernism?

A. *Rossi:* Yes, what is modernism? I believe that this invention of 'modernism', as applied to architecture, is a critical distortion related to a certain time in the history of architecture. Does one still ask oneself in painting, literature or the cinema if a work of art is modern? If a film is modern or not? In painting, the ridiculous criticisms that posed the question whether Picasso or De Chirico is modern are now irrelevant. The question is rather if one is really dealing with art and artists who are able to express themselves in a certain manner. In architecture, however, this absurd question is still of importance. Does a patient ask himself if his doctor is modern or not? It is more important to establish that a contemporary doctor practises modern medicine and can naturally prefer certain methods of healing to others. When I answered that I cannot be postmodern because I was never modern, I simply wished to state that I was simply an architect and practised this profession, just as architects have always done. It would perhaps be more logical to ask questions about style, that is to say, to ask oneself if a certain architect tends to be more 'Baroque' or more 'Renaissance'. That is a difficult question today because the boundaries between various styles are no longer clearly defined. To go back to medicine: is it not utterly absurd to ask whether a certain doctor is modern or postmodern, while it is certainly justifiable to ask which form of medicine he practises?

B. Huet: While you were just speaking, I could not help but think of Roland Barthes' attitude when he said: 'I suddenly no longer cared whether I was modern or not.' To which aspect of history are you referring to when you say that you have never been modern?

A. Rossi: I am referring to the journalistic use of the term 'modern', related to a certain 'modern' aspect of architectural history, that I question the validity of. I am convinced that there is a continuity in architecture taking place within the course of time. It is clear that Greek architecture influences that of the Renaissance, which, in turn, precedes twentieth-century architecture, etc.

Let us, however, leave this question aside as it arises from an intellectual debate, limited to certain university and journalistic circles. It loses all relevance in a country such as the United States because such superfluous questions, as you know, are hardly taken account of, except by a handful of critics in New York. In some states one encounters Georgian houses, in others, buildings made of glass. American architecture is a conglomeration of all of this.

B. Huet: This question is naturally of little importance for mass produced architecture. For the architectural elite it is a different matter, as it must have a way of 'differentiating' in one way or another, in order to survive as an elite. To a certain extent you are also a part of this.

A. Rossi: No, because I do not believe in the existence of an architectural elite. Let us return to the example I cited earlier – what is the significance of the fact that, in a large country such as America, all types of architecture exist without anyone complaining? In actual fact, the disease of modernism (or at least one of its diseases, resulting in the ruin of large areas of our cities) is its moralising, that is to say the intrusion of the question of morality into the architectural sphere. Regrettably, we still suffer from this disease today. When I say that I am not modern I am declaring my rejection of moralising in architecture, a moralising that rages like this in no other artistic discipline. One should not, at this point, start debating academic or philosophical issues. If one finds a Doric column beautiful or ugly, if one likes it or not, that is a decision that has nothing to do with morals. One accused me of demonstrating a liking for Stalinist architecture over many years, simply because I found several buildings from this time wonderful, and I still do.

Stalin had buildings constructed with columns and therefore all of Soviet architecture should not be rejected simply because of its use of columns and gables. Yet a supposedly democratic Europe regards an architectural style as democratic (and it is moreover hideous), simply because it made use of glass and built roofs that have regular, flat roofs sloping towards all sides! This is where my debate starts out from. Of the so-called 'modern' architects, it was Mies van der Rohe who influenced me the most, although he used a lot of steel and glass in the last years of his life. On the other hand, a Renaissance palace can also have a great influence on me. Architecture forms a unity, in my opinion. I make use of what is good, wherever I can find it.

Cara Architettura!

Hans Gerhard Hannesen

In his essay discussing the fragmentary, it is almost as if Aldo Rossi wants to cry out the words *Cara Architettura!*, such is his passion for architecture. 'After all, as the subject matter, the development, the relatively short lifespan of architecture is so human and moving, we cannot but lend our full attention to it.'[1] A short while ago, he inscribed the words 'The joy of building!' (*Bauen ist eine Lust!*) on the surface of some of his drawings (in German). Such enthusiasm belies the anxiety of an architect perturbed both by the destruction of the European city and the state of architecture. For many years, Rossi has played an active role in this heated debate, as there are, of course, numerous ways of judging the quality of cities and of their architecture, as well as of devising solutions.

I shall begin by taking several essential points from Rossi's writings. Other concepts will become clearer in the discussion of architectural examples. Due to the importance of Rossi's writings, it is also helpful to include a number of quotations. Since Rossi has, apart from his early theoretical texts, written some wonderfully poetical texts right up to the present day, his language grew richer with time; this proves to be highly enjoyable. This body of work, together with his drawings, gives us a much deeper understanding of his character and architecture.

Apart from numerous writings published since 1956, Rossi's most important theoretical work on architecture is *The Architecture of the City*,[2] which appeared in 1966. In this, he defines architecture not only as consisting of single buildings or as visible cityscapes with ensembles of structures, but more as a process of building, a development in the course of time.[3] It is in this manner that he proceeds to analyse the city. Similar to Robert Venturi in his book *Complexity and Contradiction in Architecture* (which appeared in the same year, though with diverse consequences), Rossi's aim is to historically refute functionalism. He writes provocatively 'that a functional analysis of the elements of urban planning is not only misleading but prevents us from analysing forms and hinders knowledge of the real architectural laws.'[4] Moreover, he adds: 'What I reject is merely the naive concept of functionalism in which functions define form, therefore clearly exerting a great influence on city planning and architecture.'[5] At another point, he enlarges on the fact that, 'It is true that elements of urban planning, in which function has long since disappeared, have retained their meaning for us. This meaning derives solely from their form which is a valuable constituent of the whole character of the city.'[6] In this context, he introduces the concept of permanence[7] that can be observed in historical monuments, visible signs of the past, and in the routes taken by streets, as well as in city plans. He cites several examples, such as the Palazzo della Ragione in Padua, which took on new functions when a small market hall was installed on its ground floor. It has thus remained alive. On the other hand, the Alhambra in Granada today houses neither Moorish nor Castilian kings, while still remaining the most important factor in the cityscape. Finally, he adds: 'The city of Split, growing up within the confines of Diocletian's Palace, thus finding a new use and meaning for inflexible forms, has become emblematic for this essential aspect of architecture and its relationship to the city. In this case, a maximum degree of conciseness in form is equal to a maximum degree of adaptability to various functions.'[8] He aims to contradict the widely held belief that form will arise solely from a planning of functions. 'It is essentially the forms (not only so far as they fulfil a function) that allow a city to come into being.'[9] Rossi therefore comes to the conclusion that historical monuments (the Italian *monumento* refers to a wider concept of historical and contemporary buildings than the German and will be used in this sense in the following) are of great importance, as they are bearers of the collective consciousness, objects where urban planning reaches a culminating point. Several years later, Rossi enlarges on the idea further and writes: 'It was especially in Berlin that I gained the impression that, today, the term "historical centre" denotes a much wider notion than a merely stylistic concept bound to the historical monuments and buildings of the past. Today, we also regard industrial complexes, gasometers, canals and railway-lines, that alternate with housing areas, as monumental.'[10] The liberation of architecture from the dictatorship of function should not, according to Rossi, lead to arbitrariness of design. There must always be a source that architecture draws from in the process of creation. Function plays an important role from the initial planning stage, as we have yet to describe. Important for an understanding of his architectural theory is the concept of 'typology' that he developed from Quatremère de Quincy. In his *Dictionnaire Historique de L'Architecture,*[11] de Quincy referred to the *model* as being precise and defined in advance, whereas the *type* is more open for interpretation: 'Thus, one can conclude that there is in the imitation of types nothing that feeling and spirit will not recognise.'[12] Rossi adds that typology, in the case of the city, as well as that of individual buildings, is 'the theory of elementary types that cannot be further reduced.'[13] He writes: 'I am inclined towards the conclusion that the prototypes applicable to the building of houses have remained unchanged from antiquity up until the present day. This does not mean that concrete lifestyles have not changed during this timespan, nor does it exclude numerous, dissimilar lifestyles.'[14] As will become clearer, Rossi always starts out from typology, considering it an essential basis for his architecture.

Andrea Mantegna, *Death of the Virgin*, 53 x 42 cm, *c.*1459,
Madrid, Museo del Prado

Years later, he wrote pragmatically about architecture in his *Scientific Autobiography:* 'The rational character of architecture is based on the fact that its components arise in relation to time. Earlier elements can become an integral part of new buildings. The construction of reality occurs because architecture relates to existing objects and to the city, to ideas and to history. Due to these conjectures, I have elsewhere set up the thesis of the "analogous city" in which I was concerned with the theoretical basis of the architectural design.'[15] He had developed the term *analogous city* in 1976, a development of his ideas in *The Architecture of the City*, published ten years earlier. In this widely published text, before defining the term, he once again sharply criticises urban planning after the Second World War. He stresses that he believes in revealing the connections between imagination and reality – for him this lies on a par with freedom. 'And I believe that the power of the imagination is factual ... in the power of the imaginary arising from the factual.'[16] Following this, he explains the term *analogous city* by referring to Canaletto's *View of Venice* in The Museum of Parma – of the three Palladio buildings depicted there, one remained in the planning stage and the others were constructed in Vicenza. Still, one was led to believe that one could find a familiar picture of Venice in this imaginary place. 'In my opinion this painting possesses an important historical and political meaning, even one that is progressive. Venice is presented as a city analogous to the Republic of Venice, as well as to a great modern nation: anyone can recognise themselves in the fixed and rational elements, in their own history, and can distinguish the particular characteristics of a place, a landscape, a moment. Without imaginary forces directed at the future there can be no solutions for the city as social place *par excellence.*'[17] He underlines the fact that beauty is useful[18] (in the way that beauty – beginning in the thirteenth century – became an essential criterion for the development of the Italian city) and writes that the functionalist explanation of objects being defined by their use alone has only caused impediments. Technological plans are not the future of the city, even if they bring with them the potential for a more comfortable way of life. He quotes Marinetti's dictum that trams had become the definition of the Milan of the future and of futurism. In the meantime, they have long since become antiquated. He points out that machines would always undergo rapid development, yet without playing a great role in the real life of the city. In the introduction to his catalogue, *Architetture Padane*,[19] Rossi defines Mantua as a *punto analogo* of the Po Plain, rather like a timeless object where this whole area arrives at a point of culmination. He then concentrates on Mantegna's altar painting *Death of the Madonna*[20] (illustration on p31) and writes: 'Sometimes the lagoon and the fog (that rises up from the rice fields, lakes and canals) mingle as on the painting of the Virgin's death by Mantegna; here death takes place in a closed room, but inner states are indicated by the landscape. Perhaps it is this landscape that, solely due the artist's greatness, on the one hand clearly brings over the 'pathos' of Mary's death, and on the other, encapsulates a picture of a timeless Mantua, where the history of the Po Plain, above all of the Lombard, but also that of Emilia and of the Veneto, can find its analogous position once again.'[21] The idea of the analogous city could hardly be explained in a better manner. Several years later, he writes in his *Scientific Autobiography*: 'I have always underlined the fact that places are stronger than people; a place is stronger than an event.'[22]

∗

Several geometric patterns run through Rossi's work like a *leitmotif*. He therefore writes, in the course of recalling a group of drawings from around 1970 in an essay, that he had defined several architectural elements in urban compositions or in those where they already form part of the architecture: 'The triangular gable, the column, the porticus, as well as extant elements, fireplaces, cylinders, cones – an understanding of architecture is only made possible by combining these geometric elements, aided by a familiarity with the history of their application.'[23]

Two particularly characteristic examples are presented in the following: the triangle and the column. The triangle appears in the Triennale complex in Milan in 1964, in the project for the Piazza Parma in 1964, and in the design for the public space in Segrate (illustration on p82) in 1965.[24] The only partially constructed public space included a view out onto the landscape and a wall with gate openings. Rossi writes that this underlines the fact that 'the public space is construction, a piece of architecture. Its boundaries are defined by cylindrical elements, fragments of another architecture. The most important element is the Memorial for the Partisans: it is composed of various architectural elements and pieces.'[25] It consists of an open-ended cube enclosing a stairway; roughly on its first third, lies a three-cornered prism that leads to a column in the manner of a roof and juts out over this. (According to the plan, water is to flow from the triangle into a basin.) Deeper levels of meaning, however, are soon made apparent in this pure geometry. One can detect a connection to the section of the *Essai sur L'Architecture* by the Jesuit priest Marc-Antoine Laugier, dating from 1753[26]. Laugier develops a programme of logical construction from the paradigm of the *petite cabane rustique*, defining supports, rafters and gables (corresponding to columns, entablatures and pediments in classical architecture) as essential components of architecture. 'If each of these three elements finds itself at the right place and in an appropriate form, there is nothing one could add to make the work complete'[27] (illustration on p35). The 'perfect triangle' of Pythagorean tradition is the first and simplest geometric figure, a mythical and magical symbol in Antiquity and the Middle Ages, that also played a highly important role in the geometric architectural orders of the Renaissance. The triangle is the symbol of the Christian Trinity, having numerous further connotations in other cultures. It lies on a par with the tetrahedron as the first regular shape which, according to Plato, expresses the beauty and variety of the world. Peter Eisenman[28] interprets the monument in Segrate both as house and coffin, therefore becoming a symbol of death.[29] The well thus becomes a well of life and the monument refers not only to the past but to the present and to the future, to the cycle of life and death. Henceforth, the triangle is found again and again in Rossi's projects, both as a well and in schools and public spaces, and also in the form of a roof, carried by supports. Similarly, it can be found in the design of a small public space in Milan, that resulted from the building of an entrance stairway for a recently constructed underground station, Croce Rossa (illustration on p152). Rossi refers back to his incompleted design for the Memorial for the Partisans in Cuneo (1962) that has retained its validity for him. At the time, he had planned a large hollow cube measuring twelve metres. A stairway, tightly enclosed by walls tapering inwards and by a heavy roof, was to have led to a heightened inner space or square, cut off from the outside and with a view only to the sky. Opposite this, he planned a window encompassing the complete width – or rather an observation vent, through which one could view the fields of the partisan battles on the hills. One can interpret the cube in its geometric simplicity as a symbol of the beginning as well as of the end of Rossi's architecture. In Milan, twenty-six years later, Rossi places a hollow cubic form, with a side open to allow for a stairway leading to a raised platform, on one side of a public space surrounded by lanterns, mulberry trees and granite benches, as is customary in the Mediterranean. He again introduces an elongated window, through which the view onto the lively comings and goings of this elegant shopping area appears strangely distanced and broken. On this side, he introduces a large triangle forming a water spout – the monument becomes a well. Water flows into a grid that is carefully embedded into the flagstones and from there, underneath the monument, into a drain that leads to the public space. Here, once again, we find the symbolism of the well of life, perhaps even as a pointer to the name of the public space (Red Square). The cube is constructed solely of coloured, grained Candoglia marble, also used to build Milan Cathedral. Rossi's comparatively modest project also brings to light his ideas on city planning and in this case he attempted to invest a place with a special significance. The complex asserts itself in an autonomously impressive manner vis-à-vis the lively to-and-fro of the shopping streets, at the same time remaining an important point of reference for the surrounding area. Unlike Richard Serra, for example, who creates an irritating effect on his surroundings with both the material and form of his huge steel sculptures, Rossi's monument possesses a typological relationship to the city and especially to Milan through the use of Candoglia marble. The monument was dedicated to former Italian State President Sandro Pertini after he had died.

Long rows of triangles form the roofs of the single dwellings in the design for the

Petite Cabane Rustique,
frontispiece from *Essai sur L'Architecture*
by M-A Laugier, 1755

student hostel in Chieti (1976) in which the layout reminds one of a Carthusian monastery with its single houses, also of a housing estate. The 'large house' or community house is found in the middle of the complex, that is to say on the site of the church. Complexity is avoided, while individuality and community are designated their clearly ascribed areas.

The triangle also appears on a comparatively minor building as, for example, on the entrance facade of the Japanese interior design firm *Ambiente,* in Tokyo (1989), where the jutting roof is composed of two powerful columns, carrying a triangular tympanum. It is typical for Rossi to use a form such as this, as he wishes to convey the idea of an exhibition building as a place where one can see everyday objects that, in sharp contrast to usual ideas of quick consumption, are meant to become universal objects of everyday life.

Rossi has also designed a 'cupboard in the form of a beach cabin' with a triangular hood that has been produced in several colourful versions, as well as in wood. It almost seems as if he creates these examples of furniture and kitchen appliances in order to playfully try out geometric forms. He therefore gives a kettle the form of a cone, a shape created by rotating a right-angled triangle and the espresso pot *la conica,* a cylindrical form on which a cone is placed as a lid. These are objects of our everyday life that, despite the attempts of numerous designers, is almost impossible to invent anew and which Rossi defines as a typologically derived elementary form. In his drawings, we sometimes find these pots placed near the houses of a city and they thus become timeless monuments, as does the espresso pot *la cupola,* that can be found self-confidently standing near a church dome. Rossi writes of his intense relationship with objects: 'I have undoubtedly always had an interest in objects, tools, machines and utensils. For this reason, I stood in the large kitchen in 'S' on Lake Como and drew coffee pots, pans and bottles for hours on end. I especially liked the blue, green and red enamelled coffee pots because they had a bizarre volume; this was the reduction of fantastical architecture that I was later to encounter. Up until the present day, I love drawing these large coffee pots, as if they were brick buildings drawn in section, with interiors I imagine it is possible to enter.'[30] Following this small aside, I should like to continue by discussing the cylindrical form.

The 'giant column' is without doubt one of the most frequently found elements on many of Rossi's monuments and buildings, and can be seen, combined with the triangle, as an essential element of his architecture. Rossi considers it one of the ever-recurring topoi of his architecture. Klotz's description of the monument of Segrate refers to both the plinth on which the cylindrical columns stand, as well as to the fact that the only partially realised plan included several cylinders on plinths. 'In this manner a breath of the historical, of the presence of the historical, is draped over the whole design.'[31] Rossi himself referred to ideas inspired by the *Ca' del Duca* in

Venice, built by Filarete (1400-69) for the Duke Francesco Sforza of Milan in 1461 but which remained unfinished. This had been incorporated into a nineteenth-century building and only a fragment of the magnificent diamond-pointed ashlars remains; the corner of the building is emphasised by an indented column (illustration on p49). Concerning this matter, he writes: 'It has always appeared to me that this insertion or relic of time, in its absolute formal purity, is a symbol of architecture engulfed by the life around it.'[32] It becomes for him both a symbol of architecture, as it encapsulates the whole concept of the palace, and a relic of time, that has remained fragmentary and is, at the same time, a symbol of the whole. Rossi's use of columns has aroused strong controversy, above all in Germany. The column was undoubtedly always used to underline the significance of the man who erected or owned a building, transcending its origins as a visualisation of support. Modernism rejected the column, as well as almost all of the architectural apparatus of decoration, calling it a form used to visually represent power.[33] Oechslin is correct in referring to this argument in conjunction with the controversy surrounding Rossi's design for the Museum of German History in Berlin 'as it is above all in Germany that solving the problems of representative building has, almost for generations, merely been considered casually, or has been ignored altogether.'[34] Giorgio Grassi writes with great pessimism: 'The modernists held the illusory belief that "new forms" of architecture could provide new content'.[35] Rossi has always rejected the ideological content of modern architecture. In sharp contrast to many architects and artists who believed they could create a better society by making a complete break with the past, Rossi always spoke of the achievements of past centuries with great reverence. He has also always believed that nothing really new could be invented. He chooses examples from Antiquity to the present to illustrate his discussions of the phenomena of architecture and urban planning and also speaks of the city as home. He does not, however, aim to revitalise historical architecture, although he is convinced that 'architecture must always refer to a source'.[36] He develops his own architectural language from the past and is convinced that its contextual meaning is in each case taken from the present as well as from the use man makes of it. In this way, the memory of previous architecture remains alive in the new.

*

Aldo Rossi's oeuvre has in the meantime become so extensive that it would be impossible to enlarge on each aspect of his rich body of work which also contains a pictorial element. The following should not be seen as a chronology of designs and buildings but rather as a discussion, using project examples and based on typology, of developments and constants, of influences and characteristics.

The housing block in Gallaratese (1969-70; illustration on p84) is one of Rossi's first major projects. It has been interpreted as the theory of rationalism transformed into architecture, not least because of the publication of a distorted drawing of the complex in the catalogue he published for the XV Triennale di Milano of 1973 in which he outlines rationalism.[37] The complex was created in conjunction with a large living area planned by, and partially also realised by, Carlo Aymonino. Rossi's building is in sharp contrast to the dramatic movement of Aymonino's architecture. It refers to the beginnings of modernism, but reaches significantly beyond it, in order to make it useful once more for solving contemporary problems. While making the plans, he took the typology of residential areas into consideration and discovered the pergola house as an antique type that has retained its significance up until the present.[38] He comes to regard these arcades as internal streets. Although he had used the prototype of the inner courtyard complex to inspire his design of a residential area in San Rocco, Monza in 1966,[39] he now finds the connection with typical Milanese working-class areas to be of significance. In its initial planning stage, the 180 metre long residential area is subdivided into two sections by a division through the middle. Instead of the square windows he originally designed and which were then custom-ary, one finds oblong windows that will become characteristic for Rossi, although supports are not accentuated here. At the point where both buildings meet, there appear four huge columns, festive prototypes of supports, instead of the usual upright supports. He has transformed the elements of silent architecture, that would otherwise have fulfilled all expectations of modernity and hygiene, into a monument. A modern residential building has been turned into a rational one.[40]

In the following years, Rossi built many rows of terrace houses and multi-family dwellings, and the following refers to several smaller houses before a larger complex, the house in Berlin's southern Friedrichstadt, is discussed. Here, once again, he is trying to find a universal solution, rather than making experiments that concern the architecture of the city only marginally. The design of house types and their ground plans refers back to highly thorough studies of domestic architecture.

In 1973, he created the design for the terrace houses in Broni that, with their gardens and areas for farming equipment, refer to the housing estates of the first third of the twentieth century, eg to Heinrich Tessenow's designs for Hellerau, near Dresden (1909). Similarly, the terrace house in Mozzo near Bergamo (1977) seems to refer to the House Monument in Segrate with its triangular rafters over the entrance stairway. The plain semi-detached houses in Goito (1979) are ennobled by triangular rafters, while the Union Building in Pergognaga of the same year is enclosed by a portico with pillars, that cannot deny its origins in the traditional buildings of the Lombard and Emilian countryside.

Recently, in his plans for a residential area with eighty two-family houses in

Cassamassima near Bari (1991), Rossi referred to Greek colonial cities by constructing a city wall with a gate area, enclosing the whole city. This was to lend it individual character among the newly built quarters of the port that had expanded rapidly around it. He writes admiringly of the beauty of Apulian farm buildings, counting them among the most cultivated (*civile*) of man's possible modes of living. Referring to this, he develops a type of semi-attached house with an inner courtyard, pergola, loggia and roof terrace. He consciously differentiates between the two house facades: towards the street, two corner towers frame a simple, almost austere facade while on the more private garden side, with its huge half-columns and moulding made of local tuff, the large windows create a connection with nature, reminiscent of the country villas of Apulia.

Simple one-family dwellings are seldom found in Rossi's oeuvre. In 1960, he built a villa in Versilia, consisting of simple, white stuccoed cubes, very much in the style of Adolf Loos, while the holiday home in the Ticino (1975), found in many variations on numerous drawings, was solely constructed as a guest cottage. In 1981, he designed a villa for the Roman Campagna which has a rectangular ground plan and a central atrium, standing wholly in the classical tradition. It was not until 1988 that he was to build two single one-family houses again – this time in Pennsylvania (illustration on p144). They pay tribute to the wooden houses of New England, that became characteristic of the entire United States, and at first sight they blend in unobtrusively with the other buildings. It would appear that Rossi only sees public building as important (characteristically, his own house on Lake Maggiore is one of the area's typical, old houses – unpretentious, inextravagant but far from sparse inside.) More recently in 1989, he constructed the Casa Alessi (illustration on p164) in Verbania on Lake Maggiore. In this case, he revived the traditional local building manner where houses were made from rough, unhewn stone from the area. Neo-classical and Romantic influences can also be detected in the terracotta columns and balustrades. One could even consider a direct reference to Palladio's Villa Sarego,[41] with its portico made of rusticated, Ionic columns between which a balustrade is placed. With the Casa Alessi, however, Rossi is not concerned with a colossal order. The unbroken architraves, for example, divide the three floors clearly.

The residential building in the southern Friedrichstadt in Berlin (1981) (illustration on p194) was created at the invitation of the International Building Exhibition (IBA) and was the first larger commission outside Italy. Rossi was thoroughly familiar with Berlin, as can be seen from an essay devoted to contemporary German architecture in *Casabella Continuità*.[42] He had been a guest of the German Architectural Academy in the eastern part of the city in 1961 and had been heavily involved with creating the issue of *Casabella Continuità* in 1961 devoted to residential building in Berlin.[43] Rossi also brought out a catalogue entitled *Architettura Razionale* about international architecture for the XV Triennale di Milano, in which issues relating to Berlin are discussed.[44] Later on, in 1976, he created a design for housing on both sides of the connecting canal, with stairways inside iron towers near the canal that were linked to the water by bridges. While planning for the IBA in 1981, his plea that the historical city be made central to the architectural discussions had long since become a commonly held belief. En-bloc building, that included green, partially public court-yards, had once more become a basis of the plans. In a description of his contribution, Rossi also enlarged on the history and characteristics of the German city, comparing Friedrich Weinbrenner's planning, as interpreted by Werner Hegemann, to the ideas of Karl Friedrich Schinkel. He shows preference for Weinbrenner, who mounted arcades in front of existing houses in his plans for redesigning the Kaiserstrasse in Karlsruhe, while there are no plans created by Schinkel that solve the problems of the city in a similarly effective manner. Rossi underlines the importance of building along street axes and mentions the special suitability of placing public spaces within the street system (Rondell, later Belle-Alliance-Platz, today, however, after the changes in the Sixties and Seventies, remains hardly recognisable as Mehringplatz on the street plan). These would reveal both an abstract idea and would also be capable of becoming principles of order.[45] In Rossi's competition design one finds an entire block of houses, so that the most striking element, a huge corner column on Wilhelm-/Kochstrasse would have had an equivalent on Puttkamerstrasse. This becomes much more than an emblem of the building, as it takes on the qualities of an element of urban planning, setting an unmistakable accent at an important street corner. It appears as if it had always been there and was now incorporated into the house. It has long since asserted its powerful presence between the buildings' windows – in which the individual decoration, unlike that of many contemporary architects, Rossi can be proud of. It remains, however, a timeless architectural monument and is also a metaphor for the rebuilding of the city through the IBA.

The corner column crops up again, as if in reference to Berlin, in 1982, in the administrative centre in Fontivegge, Perugia, at the corner of a large section with offices, a hotel and apartments. It was used again in 1985, in a complex of council flats in Vialba, Milan and in 1992, (illustration p132) on a smaller scale, in a business and residential building in Terni. In contrast, the street corner at the business and residential building in La Villette, Paris is characterised by a circular form in the receding building that glows out from the brick walls of the background because of its strong blue colour, indicating the post office, *Parc De La Villette*, (illustration p136) with its yellow lettering. Here once again the town planning effect is unmistakable. Rossi may have been inspired by some of Giuseppe Terragni's houses (1904-41). The buildings of the Soviet Revolution and the Zujev Club-Building in Moscow (1928-29), by Pantelemon Golossow, (1892-1945), (illustration on p41) that Rossi surely knew

Pantelemon Golossow, Zujev Club in Moscow, 1928-29

may also have served as models.

His house in La Villette stands out in the midst of an estate of new buildings very close to the Cité de la Musique, by Christian de Portzamparc, above all, because of its simplicity and traditional mansarde roof, quite consciously derived from the *hôtels particuliers* built by Georges-Eugène Haussmann.

Rossi recently devised a project for a residential and business area in the Schützenstrasse in Berlin's Friedrichstadt, (illustration p212) which is not as strange as it might appear at first glance. In spite of its proximity to the site of the former Berlin Wall, a wasteland to this day, this street is now undergoing a revival, thanks to its central position. Rossi has developed a master plan for the building area through which various architects should build in sections, taking into account the standard height for eaves in Berlin.[46] The plan includes an extant although run-down typical Berlin tenement house of the late nineteenth century, and a two-storey building of the same style. Rossi stresses the fact that he finds both the rebuilding and restoration of these structures, as well as the brand new buildings connected to them, a particularly interesting means of redesigning the area. It is in this way, and not only by preserving important historical monuments, that one can develop a link with the area's past. In this case, one is not concerned with the preservation of famous buildings but, quite on the contrary, with highly typical Berlin houses. The facade designs refer back to the tradition of Schinkel and of the Beaux-Art, which contrast with the simple building materials, such as brick and cement, actually used. Nevertheless one cannot deny that they possess their own grandeur. Hence, one can see that Rossi does not aim to be particularly original. The facades are made of iron and glass, the fruits of modern technology. The relationship manifests itself in an architectonic collage, as one can see from the facade, a direct reference to a Roman palace. Rossi writes: 'The idea of incorporating various references into the designs can also be observed in the grand masters of Berlin architecture such as Schlüter and Schinkel. This is partly why they are counted among the most studied of architects, making them of great interest for contemporary architecture.'[47] The project includes important elements relating to Rossi's theories on urban planning and architecture.

Knowing Rossi's vision of the world, it is but a short way from his residential architecture to his cemeteries. They are, in fact, profoundly close. In Italy, unlike in northern Europe, graveyards resemble houses for the dead. 'The cemetery itself is a building', writes Aldo Rossi in his description of the Modena Cemetery (1971-78), parts of which are still under construction[48] (illustration on p88). Early grave sites are typologically related to houses, he continues, referring to Etruscan and Roman graves and urns, that can have the form of houses. [49] In order to blend in with its Neo-classical neighbour, Rossi's cemetery is strictly geometrical. A row of ossuaries that form a triangle, tapering from the broad base to the narrowest final section, lies at the centre. At that point, one meets a conical tower under which is found a communal grave. The adjacent, round tower, that receives light from above, is for burial ceremonies. Inside this, one finds concentric circles of steps, leading down to a platform. In the middle of this stands a stone, closing the entrance to the grave site. Rossi allocated this space to the lonely, desperate and forgotten beings whose relationship to society had at some point broken off. 'The city builds its greatest monument for these underdogs', [50] which, like the smokeless chimney of an empty factory, points to the fact that here time stands still and all of life's activity has come to an end. On the other side of the triangle one finds, in strict, axial symmetry, a cubic building with open window sockets. This represents the incomplete and abandoned house, a metaphor of death translated into architecture, a place of memory, in which death is made manifest as a feeling without history. At the same time it is a place in which, as in antique graves, a social unity of feeling and architecture is achieved. In contrast to the charnel-houses with their individual graves, one can perceive the building as a *monumento collettivo,* in which the graves of war dead are placed. This also is a site for burial ceremonies. The conical tower or cone and the house, or rather the cube, are brought together by the connecting lane of the ossuaries. They are, so to say, linked by this backbone of the entire body, and become a monumental sign of death and remembrance, due to their scale [51]. Finally, the complex is enclosed by a large, right-angled, outer section, the columbarium. The empty areas thus created are designated for earth burials. Rossi sees the cemetery as a communal place and as an urban monument. He writes that its most important relationship to the city lies in its ability to form a *luogo architettonic,* in which the rational design of buildings are interpretations of piety and of the meaning of cemeteries – an alternative to the ugly and disorderly growth of the modern city. Several years later he remarks, pointing out the long controversies that have now been forgotten after the first burials took place: 'In order to be great, architecture must forget itself or must construct nothing more than a point of reference that melts into the memory.' [52] In this context, he also indicates Adolf Loos' comment, quoted in his book *The Architecture of the City,* as it excited him because of its Biblical character: 'If we come upon a hillock in the woods, six feet high and three feet wide, formed into a pyramid by a shovel, we become earnest and something in us says: someone lies buried here – that is architecture.' [53] The cemetery, and its buildings, however, does not remain independent of the rest of the city's architecture. It is the space the community has designated for the organisational manner of dealing with death, just as school buildings, for example, are erected to form a stage for life. Rossi connected the triangular design of the cemetery with the ground plan of the school of

Fagnano Olona of 1972,[54] adding the skeleton of a fish in such a manner that the skeleton and the head are placed near the charnel-house sections and the tower of the communal grave. The fish is an ancient fertility symbol while at the same time being a chthonic animal that is related to funerals and embodies, in the Christian sense, the hope of rebirth. It is an early Christian symbol of Christ, and in other contexts, for the community. In Rossi's drawing, it probably also symbolises the fact that architecture can only create space for the living and the dead. If one looks at the cemetery today and sees the large, simple buildings forming shadows to the rhythm of the days and seasons, the complex appears like a *pittura metafisica* by a painter such as Giorgio de Chirico.

More recently, Rossi created plans for the Ponte Seso cemetery in Rozzano in which a street, lined by trees, lamps and benches leads past the charnel-houses and a crematorium, towards an eight-cornered cemetery chapel.

Finally, one should not fail to mention the burial chapel for the Molteni family in Giussano, dating from 1980 (illustration on p108). Here Rossi no longer wished to find a universally applicable form. He wanted to create a space where a family he knows well can bury its dead and where he commemorates their prayers. The free-standing cube is decorated by a Neo-classical moulding, as are the neighbouring mausoleums. In this case, it does not run right the way around but appears only as fragments towards the back, a symbol of transitoriness. Inside, light falls through a glass roof and lights up a wooden altar in the form of Palladian gate architecture, measuring about seven metres, placed before the back wall, painted light blue.[55] The other walls are plain, the hand-made bricks solely given a structure by the steel supports carrying the roof construction. The high quality of craftsmanship found throughout the chapel speaks for the self-confidence of a family of furniture manufacturers, that continues to uphold a tradition of fine carpentry. The space can be seen as an abandoned workshop. The altar becomes both a sign of duty towards art and a doorway between life and death.

*

The Modena cemetery is undoubtedly an important monument for the city and belongs to Rossi's 'primary elements', as do all buildings discussed in this text. We now turn to a group of buildings that must be counted among these prime examples of city culture, due to their significance for urban planning and society: communal and industrial administrative centres, congress centres and sports complexes, to an airport and port design, to department stores and also to hotels which are especially important because of their position and size. Several of the projects are concerned with the design of whole city areas, possessing a variety of functions. Stubbornly defending the city as the place for cultural development – as is traditional in Italy – Rossi sees it as his responsibility to find universal formulas, just as the builders of the Middle Ages gave expression to collective experience. He regards the ever-growing problems created by the rapid expansion of the cities as a challenge that will always lead him to find new answers and solutions. In believing this, he makes it clear, however, that 'the architect does not build for a single function or timespan but simply creates the stage for what may come into being. Only second-raters believe that they can alter human emotions; on the other hand, it appears that the great historical monuments are unclassifiable, as they lie in the landscape's interior and in the history of the human race.'[56]

Rossi's early design for the Scandicci town hall (1968) reveals important characteristics of the work that was to come later. While he could hardly allow the Gallaratese block of houses to become conspicuous among the surrounding buildings, he was attempting to find an appropriate form for a public building possessing a variety of functions. Using 'particular constants of Tuscan architecture and industrial complexes' that are always fascinating with their 'simple, fantastic forms, chimneys, reservoirs, cupolas, bridges etc'[57] as inspiration, he designed an ensemble composed of various geometric shapes, linked to one another by a metal bridge. He writes about one of the design sketches: 'The relationship to the garden is particularly important; I have made use of a reference in order to underline this. The meandering path is taken from a drawing Schinkel made for a country house at Charlottenhof, Potsdam, connecting the building with the wood. This reference to Schinkel seemed to me more appropriate than an interpretation would have been.'[58] One should add that his interest in the Potsdam country house certainly also stems from Schinkel's examination of Pliny's villa description.[59]

It is a different matter with the large complex of the Triest regional government (1974). In this case, it was important to integrate the new building that was on a slope into the strict street system of the densely built-up area of Triest near the harbour. Rossi emphasised several times how moved he was by the bright sunlight in this city by the sea.[60] The project envisaged two elongated blocks, that were to be connected in the middle by three halls extending over all three floors, in which entrances, steps and lifts were to be found. While both wings of the building with their square windows do not demonstrate a particular structure, the middle is emphasised by four huge columns and three triangular pediments. A 'modern' building in the style of Otto Salvisberg or Ludwig Hilberseimer becomes a 'rational' one, 'the typology of a modern ribbon development is combined with that of classical architecture'[61]. In this context, it is interesting to take note of a design sketch where Rossi varies several roof forms and schematically draws a high cupola over the middle of the three roofs.[62] He attempts to replace the historical form by a modern equivalent that he found here in

45

the triangular-shaped roof of the prototype of the hut.

A triangular pediment, this time including a clock, once again marks the middle of the aforementioned administrative local government building in Perugia/Fontivegge (1982; illustration on p112). In this case, the Buitoni pasta factory and the city of Perugia formed a large collective undertaking, using the site of the former industrial quarter between the historical city centre and the business and residential areas of the post-war period. The Palazzo Regionale (that Rossi also likes to call *palazzo pubblico, palazzo dei signori, broletto* or *aregno* in the tradition of Italian cities), with its huge slabs, has an E-shaped ground plan. The middle wing that is narrower, and juts forth slightly and has a wide entrance stairway, is accentuated by a high portico and a triangular pediment. Opposite, lies an elongated building housing offices, shops and apartments in which the corner column has already been referred to. The wide, open space between the buildings is subdivided by a fountain in the same manner as the Segrate complex. A small theatre can be found in front of this section that is about double as long as the Palazzo Regionale. Underneath the whole complex is a garage. One should point out several further characteristics of the complex: a factory chimney that was a last relict of the old pasta factory[63] remained standing – its inclusion must have been highly significant for Rossi as a reminder of industrialisation and a symbol of the worker's movement. For these reasons, and also to erect an architectural landmark, he had additionally referred to the factory chimney in other projects.[64] In Perugia, the street that leads under the Palazzo Regionale into the underground garage faces the chimney. Rossi, following Italian urban tradition, evened out the steep, sloping site of the buildings with an ascending base, reminding one of the rusticated ground floors of past centuries. The space is incorporated into the local topography, as is often the case in Umbria, the Marche or in Tuscany. The conical entrance tower of the theatre, that can also be used for exhibitions and conferences, as it is a multi-purpose building, forms the optical centre. The clear structuring of the new centre's entire area, as well as the careful treatment of stone, which includes the flagging of the public space, should upgrade the dilapidated industrial area, providing a connecting link with the important historical heart at the higher old part of town. Rossi writes of Perugia with its net of streets, public spaces, historical monuments and apartments, business buildings and the *pubbliche istruzione* (universities, schools, libraries), describing it as being 'close to the perfect model for the Italian city'.[65]

The ideal of the historical city underlies Rossi's other projects concerned with urban planning, although one can discern of course particular typological relationships to the place in question. An example is his new design for a residential quarter in the Giudecca in Venice (1985). Here, leading out from the gardens of the *zitadelle,*[66] a *campo*[67] is formed by four-storey houses and an inner ring of lower buildings, followed by a second, more central, *campo* and finally by a *calle* leading onto the

Giotto, *St Francis Expelling the Demons from Arezzo*,
c.1296, Assisi, San Francesco

existing Calle di Michelangelo via comb-like, jutting-out wings, subdivided by *vicoli*.

In the plans for the Bicocca area in Milan (1986), Rossi attempted to construct a new city quarter near the old railway which included a technology centre, a park with a man-made lake, a garden space between the railway-lines unusual in the regular layout of a city, as well as a complex containing cultural and leisure facilities (greenhouses, museums, libraries, restaurants) incorporated into the interior of the old railway-station.

In a sketch for a business and shopping area in the Schlachthuis area of The Hague (1988), Rossi acknowledges traditional Dutch urban planning in his design for a square-perimeter layout with a courtyard development showing terraced street fronts and a green, inner public space, linked to the old pieces of land.

Rossi takes particular consideration of the historical situation of the city in the new complex of buildings in Città di Castello (1990). He will exert great influence on a place whose history means much to him by carrying out his plans for the new local administrative headquarters which includes gardens, apartments, shops and a shopping and business area. He writes: 'The Italian cities grew up as free communities and the houses were closely linked to the cathedral, schools and community areas.'[68] The town hall has a facade that faces the railway station lying opposite. A public space is formed by three of the building's wings, surrounded by arcades on the ground floor. A protruding slab runs through the main wing of the house and also emphasises the middle of the facade by means of a triangular gable. A diagonally placed avenue connects the town hall with the old city centre. A garden with groups of trees and houses on two sides is found opposite. On the fourth side, one finds a large department store, clearly subdivided into individual sections in imitation of various prototypes which thus blends in with the scale of the old city.

Having discussed several of these complexes, an important part of Rossi's views on urban planning, I shall now return to a single building, the town hall of Borgoricco (1983; illustration p116). Unlike the large administrative buildings discussed above, this is a relatively small community building in a new town near Mestre, located within the strict Roman system of axes where *cardo* and *decumanus* are lost in the horizons of surrounding fields. In this case, one is dealing with a general type, rather than an individual entity. Inspired by Palladian buildings and industrial compounds, Rossi creates a complex in which the various functions of the town hall are strictly divided and are discernible from the outside. The centre with its portico, emphasised by two huge round columns and an iron architrave, is influenced by the prototype of the villa. Here one finds the publicly accessible areas: foyer, offices of the council representatives, an exhibition hall and a library. The large assembly room on the top floor has a timbered vault, typical for historical buildings in the Veneto, derived from ship building. The main building and both side wings, with their arcades, form a small

Venice, corner column on the Ca' del Duca,
Antonio di Pietro Averlino (Filarete), 1461

piazza, open on the fourth side. On the foremost sides of these sections, in which the administrative offices are housed, one finds two fountains of life, that have been encountered before in Rossi's oeuvre. A factory chimney above the heating complex emphasises the middle axis on the back side of the strictly symmetrical body of the building. The town hall belongs to the group of Rossi's buildings that have been realised using elements that he constantly redraws. In this manner, the sketched ideas could then be realised and it is therefore a particularly significant work of these years.

Numerous poetic, architectural drawings are particularly enlightening for an understanding of the artist-architect Aldo Rossi's oeuvre. In these urban visions, the same buildings are found again and again, but are combined in new ways, are confronted by new buildings or melt into a unity. It appears as if Rossi draws strength from these works of art in order to find solutions for concrete, architectural problems.

Rossi similarly develops a strictly symmetrical complex for the design for a congress centre in Milan (1982): he starts with a tower that is round, free-standing and crowned by a circular cone as the roof, inside of which one finds a round conference room. This is a reference to the architecture of Claude-Nicolas Ledoux and, more importantly, to that of Etienne-Louis Boullée,[69] who is also referred to in other designs.[70] This is followed by a gallery leading across all floors on both sides connected to four office sections in a comb-like manner and finally by a quadratic high-rise in which the conference halls are to be found. However, as the construction of the congress centre did not come about because of local politics, Rossi was asked to create a second design in 1990 (illustration on p178). In this case, he tackled the problem by making use of the architectural history of Milan in a significant manner. In an explanatory report, he writes: 'Architecture follows many paths, but the initial stage of a creation must encompass the ideal relationship from which further developments can arise so that its own form of expression can be found.'[71] In the case of the congress centre, this is provided by the memory of the *aregno*, the *arengario* and the Palazzo della Ragione. The impressive communal city palaces of the Late Middle Ages in which the citizens gathered, are, today, often still the centres of many north Italian cities and were self-assuredly meant to provide a counterpoint to the church, or feudal palace. They are a particularly forceful expression of the urban culture of free citizens, as this is where the town's business matters were discussed. Rossi writes that most of the congress centres he has seen are ugly, and that this occurs because one has forgotten the roots of their existence, which is, in fact, the tradition of independent citizens and free speech. Naturally, what impresses the visitor reaches beyond the comfortable chairs, the colour combinations or the highly developed quality of the sound system, as all this is a matter of course and in fact always lies slightly behind the actual state of technological progress. The exalted structuring of technology moreover, always seems somewhat ridiculous in comparison to the state of its development. Therefore,

Rossi deems it necessary that a congress centre not only keeps up with the latest technology, but that it also continually adapts itself to the most recent technical changes.[72] I consider this indication by Rossi of the importance of technology as being of great significance. In an interview, Rossi once stated: 'My initial association of ideas for a project is always linked to classification, to construction and to technological problems. I despise so-called utopian architecture. I am an extremely realistic architect, highly job-oriented ... One finds an outline of the main problems facing the construction of a building in the initial sketches ... While drawing, I always have the possibility of construction in mind; after this, further layers of reality can be added.'[73] His design envisages an austere complex, reminding one of Medieval fortresses, which opens out onto an elevated, grass public space, surrounded by a two-storey colonnade, from the middle of which rises a high factory chimney. The tower is one of the last relics of the former industrial city, as the Alfa Romeo factory once stood here and will, according to Rossi, be united with the old *arengario* in the course of time. He goes on to add: 'It appears to me that it is indeed possible to create a work of our time from these memories and inspirations that will become, like all great architecture, timeless.'[74]

Rossi starts out with vastly diverging town planning prerequisites for the Casa Aurora in Turin (1984; illustration on p124),[75] the business headquarters of the textile company consortium GFT,[76] which counts important dress designers among its employees. The capital of Piedmont is an administrative, industrial and merchant city, that grew up according to a strict plan. Its large Baroque and Neo-classical centre is dominated by a unified, compact architectural structure with arcades running on the ground level. Therefore, the Casa Aurora, which lies on a street corner, also has an L-shaped ground plan and arcades in which openings are framed by double T-irons painted green, long since a characteristic element of Rossi's architecture. The supports and the floor above, with its square windows made from local stone, form a type of support zone for the upper brick floors. These have a pattern of vertical windows that are double as thick, separated by a classical moulding. The roof area has dormer-windows, typical for Turin, but seldom found in the rest of Italy. Each wing of the building ends in a windowless, tower-like structure, in which entrances are to be found. The typical and unmistakable characteristic of the building is the corner facade, a windowless brick tower that runs through the building and in which two huge columns and a green iron architrave mark the entrance. Apart from the relationship to Turin, the Casa Aurora also reminds one of the famous Viennese residential and business building, Goldmann & Salatsch, by Adolf Loos, because of the special treatment of the ground floor, and the emphasis on corners through the use of columns and architrave – it is highly likely that the Goldmann & Salatsch building, as an exclusive fashion salon, may also have been an inspiration for this one. On the upper floor of the corner tower one can find a small theatre. Its brick front wall opens up into a stage, framed by two white columns and a green architrave, a reference to the facade. Four windows above this give the impression of it being an outer wall. The iron bracing of the glass roof reminds one of industrial buildings while the beautifully patterned parquet flooring and the side walls of smooth marble stucco are characteristic of elegant interiors. These details of this simple room, however, only become apparent at second glance. The elements of *salon* and *piazza* are combined attractively. Fashion shows take place here. At the same time, Rossi discounts the possibility of ignoring the work actually done here. He entitled one of the most intensively detailed drawings of the Casa Aurora, which connects his structure with important emblematical buildings of the city, Theatrum Sabaudiae[77](see illustration on p124), in the manner of a metaphor for the city. In the meantime, Rossi has worked on filling the still empty part of the area with houses and business buildings (for the same client).

If one takes into account the numerous business and administrative buildings that were designed in the following years, and which one cannot all name in this context, one is impressed by the constant recurrence of new ideas. In each design, however, the architecture's signature is unmistakable and there are valid reasons for the amalgamation of single buildings that arise from each individual situation. Thus, the design for the administrative building of the Swiss Union Bank in Manno near Lugano (UBS/SBG; 1991) envisages a complex composed of various wings enclosing a quadratic inner courtyard, accentuated by four corner towers, as well as a yard which opens towards the front, and a high, hipped or barrel roof. Rossi again envisages a circular conference room, its entrance facing the inner courtyard.

The contract given to Rossi for the design of an office complex for the Disney Development Company in Orlando (1991; illustration on p184), although this was to be outside the actual Disney complex, is a sign that the company consciously distanced itself from a corporate identity with its idea of architecture as entertainment. Rossi refers to the origins of American cities, and also goes back to European public spaces, such as the Piazza dei Miracoli in Pisa.[78] He thus creates three diverse, large administrative buildings surrounding an area of grass. The design for the administrative building for EuroDisney in Paris (1991) envisages three diverse houses structured in a parallel manner. These surround a central, main tower and are unified by Rossi's use of exactly the same building materials and design details.

The large business, shopping and residential complex in Kuala Lumpur, Malaysia (1991) is dominated by four skyscrapers connected to shops and restaurants, located on a common ground floor area. They open out onto a water basin, leading to a river. This basin is divided in two by a type of pier, on which a further multi-storey building is found. Rossi was fascinated by this country, by the clash of the present ultra-modern with an old, Oriental culture which has Islamic, as well as Chinese and Indian elements. He considers it vital to form a link with local stylistic elements, as 'the International Style has destroyed the characteristic elements of many European, Asiatic and American cities'.[79] One can therefore discern various elements taken from local architecture in the design. At the end of the pier, he has included a reference to Venice, the Dogana,[80] that, in its original version, points towards the East and should therefore symbolise the bridge between Orient and Occident, between the Christian and Islamic world.

In his plans for a business and services centre in the Landsberger Allee[81] in East Berlin (1992; illustration on p208), he is attempting to mark the transition from an area still characterised by nineteenth-century buildings to a post-war residential one. This lies on one of the largest arterial roads of the city, where wide railway-tracks form a type of caesura between the two areas. The brick buildings of the former butchery, which is to be given a new function, indicate the industrial importance of Berlin in former days. In contrast to the aforementioned project on the Schützenstrasse in Berlin, where the aim was to reconstruct an area of the old city, it is in this case necessary to build in a manner that will stand up against the monotony of the adjacent, modern quarter. Rossi's main facade faces Landsberger Allee and a high tower emphasises the corner at the adjoining Storkower Strasse. As this can be seen from far away, it becomes a point of orientation for the street-crossing. This is also an important traffic junction, due to its urban railway station, as well as its bus-stops and tram-stops. It has up until the present, however, been without any urban landmark – also necessary for socio-psychological reasons – that would have made it a place with its own, distinct character. Rossi forms a link with traditional city architecture by building courtyard structures with compact street fronts, with shops on the ground floor. The green, inner spaces, shielded from street noise, become a place of rest and recuperation.

After citing this group of public and private administrative and shopping complexes, we turn to the Palazzo dello Sport in Milan (1988; illustration on p156), which is a 'primary element' of the city. Here, once again, Rossi regards it as an important part of his work to upgrade a neglected area by building a large, public complex. He writes of the plans for a sports complex in Palermo (1987): 'Large structures can release the peripheries from their fate as dormant cities or residential ghettos ... The architecture of the Modern movement, especially degenerate during the Sixties, has destroyed the continuity of the city because of its functional inflexibility.'[82] The initial sketches connect Milan's significant historical monuments, such as the Cathedral, the Castello Sforzesco and San Siro Stadium to Rossi's own building, by means of the required scale. He writes: 'I have for some time been concerned with large dimensions (of buildings) and with the interdependence of quality and size; buildings should tolerate no stylistic affectations; here the most important details are the cut and quality of the stone, the iron of the beams, the stairs and the main stairway, as well as the parking lots and trees that I imagine being like the rows of mulberry trees on the Po Plain.'[83] Once again, the complex is structured by towers that are like the fortresses on a ring of walls. One therefore receives an impression of the city not unlike that found in medieval altar paintings.

In his plans for the Milan-Linate airport (1991; illustration on p180), Rossi again calls into question the meaning of such a complex for the system of the city. He compares airports with the ports and railway-stations that formerly provided the first picture of the city. They are modern city-gates but are also like autonomous cities because of their constant growth. Rossi is therefore highly concerned that the perception of the complex should become lost in the existing indecipherability of the airport. He decides on a facade facing the starting and landing track, structured by columns. The glass walls found in-between are transformed into windows by green frames. The borders of the large gates and the pedestrian bridges are yellow.

In a project for the port area of Zeebrugge (1989), he is inspired by the idea of a *stazione marittima* and creates a huge tower which is a landmark for those crossing the Atlantic.

As has already been mentioned, Rossi describes the city as a space for living in which the 'primary elements' are highly important. This is not so much due to their functions, which change in the course of time, as one can easily discern in historical buildings, as because of their sentimental value and their position in the cityscape. This confrontation is important during each new project. The medieval cities of Italy had important market halls, just as stories relate to the unique, mystical character of Oriental bazaars. The great galleries of the nineteenth century became symbols of urban life while modern department stores and passages take their cue from these associations. In designing the shopping centre Centro Torri near Parma (1985; illustration on p128), found in the midst of the austere, flat Lombard landscape, Rossi opts for a complex in which the main element is a row of twelve towers, on which one finds inscribed the name Centro Torri. Once again, the creation of the modern building forms a link with the ancient cityscape, with the towers of the town hall and palaces of the ruling families, as well as the church spires, encountered in many Italian cities. Rossi was able to convince the clients, a farm production union, of the idea of leaving the sides of the corner towers open. This provides space for advertising boards and electric signs, thus adding a contemporary accent.

In the shopping centre at Gifu, Japan, (1988) it was necessary to create an easily discernible, modern centre in a monotonous area, lying outside the important historic city centre with its temples and palaces. Therefore, Rossi envisages the new structure taking over the role of ancient buildings. In the final version of the project, one finds a

Arezzo, Pieve di Santa Maria, first quarter of the 13th century

simple building with large gates and a tower, on which the name of the company is inscribed. The business centre Tochi in Nagoya, Japan, (1989) is tackled in a similar manner. Here, Rossi uses the construction of antique cities as inspiration. They were planned according to a strict scheme while still allowing great variety within individual building lots.[84]

In the meantime, Rossi has also completed several further projects in Japan. Perhaps the most important of these buildings within his architectural oeuvre is the hotel Il Palazzo in Fukuoka (1987; illustration on p140), whose name appears quite programmatic. The hotel lies in a muddle of miscellaneous buildings in a lively port area and should add to the upgrading of the area. The facade impressively dominates the surroundings. Rossi himself writes that he came upon the idea for creating this while designing the Palestra at Olginate, Como (1987), whose facade is structured by a row of columns with an architrave. In this case he piled one portico over the other. In so doing, he could also be referring to the blind arcades on medieval church facades. As is the case with the facade of the Pieve in Arezzo dating from the twelfth/thirteenth century (illustration, p55), that of the baptistry in Parma (illustration, p57) or those of many churches of Pisa or Lucca, the facade in Fukuoka is put in front of the actual building. This seven-storey structure appears to be inserted into the two side walls, in front of a windowless marble wall, by means of columns of red marble and the familiar green, steel architraves. It is crowned by a huge, protruding green cornice over which the marble wall appears like an attic storey. Three doors lead into the building, while windows can only be found at the sides. The facade is more than just the entrance side of the hotel. It has taken on an important urbanistic function, is *scenae frons* and transforms the elevated, frontal space into a stage, a *proscenium*. The dimensions of the older buildings are taken up by two low side wings (*paraskenien*) with their pointed roofs flanking the main building. They face the street, blind gables rising above the roof while the middle of the building is emphasised by a tower. The two lanes, created by this structuring of the buildings, lead into the background in a way comparable to Mannerist stage architecture. They also cut through the complex and form a connection with the surrounding lanes. The outer facade is referred to once again in the end wall of the bar. Interiors are connected with exteriors, as is the case with the Teatrino of the Casa Aurora, and the theatre in Genoa, which will be discussed later. Rossi refers to public spaces as 'life's stage' on which each man plays his role. In a poetic text about the project, Rossi states that it refers to other, external experiences, dimensions and voices, as do all of his larger projects. Even if it does so only in reference to those concerning architecture: 'To the demon of analogy that connects the baptistry of Parma with the Buddha-temple of Gifu and the canals of Triest with those of Fukuoka.'[85]

In the meantime, Rossi has made a version of this facade structure for a restaurant

Parma, Baptistery, 1196-1216/1260

with a beer hall in Sapporo in Hokkaido (1989), a building on a crossroads. In this case, he was also attempting to accentuate the street corner.

✳

The buildings, theatres, museums, a library and a church that will be described later all have to fulfil their representative functions in a traditional manner, as the society of a city, or even of a country, sees itself reflected in them. In several of them one can clearly discern Rossi's ideas of the fragmentary nature of our society, combined with a philosophy found throughout Romanesque culture, encountered above all in literature.[86] Rossi himself constantly comes back to this term as when he writes, for example, that 'the term "fragments" seems appropriate for a portrayal of the situation of the modern city, of architecture or of society'.[87] At another point, he continues: 'I often suddenly see buildings as if they were people; as if one could find the reasons behind their fate with the eye of a doctor. Therefore, or also because of this, I have spoken of fragments.' In a series of drawings, he combines architectural and furniture designs with horse skeletons.[88] In several texts about the fragmentary, he relates his own corporeal experiences after an accident to architecture and the term 'body of a building' (*Baukörper*) is then taken most literally. This highly sensuous relationship to architecture is particularly obvious in his description of the sculpture of San Carlone,[89] the huge bronze statue of St Carlo Borromeo from the seventeenth century dominating the countryside around Arona, near Lake Maggiore, for miles around it. One can step into it, as if entering a house and look out of its eyes, as if out of windows. He compares his own profession with that of a surgeon: 'As if the new city was made of elements, that while gaining in significance increasingly draw apart, and that these various fragments of a broken system are joined anew in the unity that we are longing for.'[90] We shall therefore discuss designs for universities and schools along with this group, as they reflect this view of the world to a certain extent, while at the same time expressing a rejection of closed ideologies and an openness that is the prerequisite for a free society. Keeping to a chronological order, we shall first discuss the schools.

In the high school of San Sabba in Triest (1968-69) the body of the building is structured austerely in strict accordance with Rossi's early rational ideas on architecture. The steep building requires a high ground floor, along which a wide stairway leads from the mountain road to the main entrance. Facing this street is a covered lane of jutting out, white columns superimposed onto the school buildings, a reference to the educational institutions of the nineteenth century.

The elementary school of Fagnano Olona (1972; illustration on p94) has already been mentioned, as Rossi contrasted its ground plan with that of the cemetery in Modena on a drawing. The entrance side is emphasised by a free-standing 'factory chimney' of red bricks. The symmetrical complex formed by buildings for classrooms, sports and other group activities, mensa and administration is grouped around the lightly stuccoed structures, each connected to one another. This forms the real centre of school life. A wide stairway leads up to a stage on the end wall. Two doors, rather than a main entrance, lead to the interior. Over these, one finds a clock. This is an utterly everyday object and at the same time an ancient symbol of time and of transience. It should warn the pupils of the dictates of time over their lives from now on. Rossi enlarges his ideas in the following manner: 'Here, time is represented in a special way; it is the time of childhood, group photos and all the practical jokes they include. The building has been transformed into pure theatre, although this is the theatre of life, even if everything has been set out in advance. For everything has already been set down in the building and this fact creates freedom. It is like a meeting, holidays, a lover's journey or countless other things that one determines in advance, so that they have the possibility of taking place. Although I love uncertainty, I have always believed that only pitiful people without imagination reject sufficient organisation. For it is only this organisation that allows incidents, variations, joys and disappointments to take place. In any case, it is true that I had a vision of this school, that is to say, this theatre with its everyday occurrences. The playful children were the house of life, the reverse side of the other great design, the burial chamber, the cemetery of Modena. One should add that this also has a life of its own and exists within time.'[91] The side of the school yard lying opposite, is accentuated by the library, a circular building. Rossi writes that in the case of the Fagnano Olona school the inspiration for his formal concepts was the idea that books should have a central position in a library, although, figuratively speaking, another point of view would have been equally viable. It is actually in the school at Broni that this point of view and its architectural solution would then lead to the creation of the school's centre.[92] This appears an important statement for an understanding of Rossi's planning where circular buildings play such an important role.

Four one-storey wings of the same size form a courtyard at the secondary school at Broni (1979; illustration on p100), in which the centre is emphasised by a two-storey, octagonal building. The entrance side is emphasised by a type of portico with openings cut out of the flat, white wall, reminiscent of the Palladio motif.[93] A clock is once again placed in the gable area. A tower with steps, like a campanile, forming the chimney of the heating system, stands near the complex which also reminds one of a monastery courtyard.

In the case of the Scuola media in Cantù (1986), Rossi designed a building in which symmetrical design is reminiscent of a skeleton. The barrel vaulted sports hall ends in an apse. Behind it, two arms and a cross-bolt, linking both entrances in the form of a passage, connect a closed courtyard with one opened towards the front. Here, he also places an emblem of the school in the form of a tower-like planetarium.

Rossi regards the main architectural problem in the design for an extension of the school of architecture of the University of Miami (1986) as the creation of a central space that should become a point of reference for further architectural developments. He consciously chooses the term 'Acropolis' for the group of buildings that includes a rotunda, a square building with corner towers and a row of houses with barrel-shaped roofs. These form a small city on a raised plinth, also serving as an underground garage. One is reminded of the planned cities of the Renaissance such as Pienza or Sabioneta. They were created, by means of feudal willpower, as small cultural centres to bring order to the world and to better man through art, retaining their impact up until the present. Rossi connects the natural site on a lake with associations of a settlement near water by using a pier. According to the original plan, the library on a platform on the water should refer to the Teatro del Mondo.

While transforming an old cotton factory in Castellanza into the Libero Istituto Universitario Cesare Cattaneo (1990; illustration on p166) Rossi became fascinated by the industrial complexes of the Olona Valley. He regarded a large part of his task as, on the one hand, forming the link between the new building, the rapidly expanded area and the historical city centre as well as, on the other hand, preserving the old buildings by providing them with a new function. The result was a highly attractive ensemble of ancient and modern buildings that create a new centre for the surrounding area, without even a hint of nostalgia, although the whole is able to keep up the standards of an old country town.

Finally, Rossi indicates a third type of university in his design for a new Polytechnic in Bari (1991). He takes the lead from the great examples of the University of Padua, dating from the fifteenth/sixteenth century, with its inner courtyard, giving an impression of Classicism, and the University of Milan, that was moved into the old Ospedale Maggiore in 1954, designed by Filarete in the mid-fifteenth century,[94] a building clearly structured around quadratic courtyards. He was also inspired by Oxford University, with its gradually enlarged structure of inner courtyards. Rossi planned a grid of courtyards of various sizes around a central, main building. Taking the Mediterranean climate into account, he concentrates largely on problems related to sunlight and ventilation.

It has become clear from the above that the term theatre is also a metaphor for Rossi's view of the world. One can conclude that his designs for the theatre are related to the world in a special manner – the architectural stage of life is as it was, brought onto the 'boards'. Rossi repeatedly writes that architecture provides the stage for public life, whereas streets and public spaces merely serve to create the space in

Etruscan urn in the form of a house, 4th century BC

which life takes place. He demonstrated this as a philosophical game in the small Teatrino Scientifico (1978),[95] where the main elements of architecture can be studied on a model stage. It is an object, lying somewhere between a machine (Rossi uses the word *macchina* which also means gadget in its widest sense), a theatre and a toy which is above all, as Rossi expresses it, 'in its most elementary form, a space for stage action as well as for experience.'[96] M Tafuri writes that Rossi's metaphysical theatre aims to convince us that 'the space for performing (*rappresentazione*) is in accordance with the representation of the space.'[97] In his *Scientific Autobiography*, he writes: 'I have been fascinated by the theatre throughout my architectural life ... The last (Teatrino Scientifico) is one of my favourite designs.'[98]

In the same year, Rossi designed a wooden theatre that can be counted among his most important creations, although it has long since been destroyed by fire, only existing in pictures or as a memory: the Teatro del Mondo (illustration on p104) floats on a ship in the water and came about within the framework of the Architecture Biennale of Venice. Despite standing in the tradition of the floating theatres, popular during carnivals of the eighteenth century, it created the impression of belonging to a dream-world in a city that, more than any other, appears to lie anchored at the seashore. Its public spaces particularly resemble theatre stages.

In the intermediate area between theatre and public space are also the designs Rossi created for open-air stages[99] with their houses, walls, gates and rooms. There is also the Teatro Domestico for the Triennale di Milano (1986) that allows one to look in at different wallpapered rooms, not unlike an enormous doll's house, including one in which large coffee pots and kettles reside as if they were real characters. One is also reminded of the wooden lighthouse-theatre in Toronto (1988; illustration on p150) that stood on the shore of Lake Ontario one summer, during the exhibition *Art in Architecture*. With its red and white striped lighthouse and the dummy house facades, it created a segment of a small model town in which drama and comedy could take turns.

The task during the building of the Teatro Carlo Felice in Genoa (1982, completed in 1990; illustration on p120) was to reconstruct the classical opera house by Barabino,[100] bombed in the last war, and to include the latest technological requirements in the plans.[101] Various attempts at reconstruction had been made since 1949.[102] What is noteworthy in the choice of Rossi's architecture is that it discounts both the confrontation of the old with a functional architectural language, typical of the Sixties and Seventies, as well as extension design that alienates the historical building (eg such as that created by Robert Venturi and Denise Scott-Brown in their extension of the National Gallery in London).[103] He is able to develop a new building, at the same time keeping a close connection to the older one. The new theatre clearly refers to its predecessor. The ruins of the side portico and marble lobby facing the Piazza Ferrari are rebuilt. A part of the older theatre is reconstructed, according to Barabino's

Sabbioneta, Galerie degli Antichi, 1583-84

drawings. In order to provide a link with the surrounding area, Rossi creates a passage from the Piazza Ferrari to the Galleria Mazzini lying behind it. This area has become part of the public thoroughfare system, as one enters the passage through the frontal hall of columns – its sacred character was thus reduced. The actual entrance to the theatre lies in the building's interior. (Here one is reminded of Schinkel's *Schauspielhaus* in which the coach driveway lay under the great main stairway. The portico with its columns could no longer be counted among the repertoire of feudal architecture but ennobled the theatre into a bourgeois place of learning. In this manner, the front of the temple has lent a new significance and restored life in a society in the throes of change.) A conical light-shaft tapering upwards leads through the four storeys of the foyer, a free-standing architectural element found frequently in Rossi's work and that, in this case, comes through the roof in the form of a glass point. (The free-standing, conical tower, forming the entrance foyer of the theatre in Fontivegge, has already been mentioned.) Rossi mentions the interior, glass-covered courtyard of the University of Zurich on several occasions, as he had studied the impression made by light on the interior of the building, according to the course of the days and seasons. He had made use of these lessons to create new architectural forms. A huge tower above the stage has in turn become a modern emblem of the city.

The interior of the theatre hall is most striking with its walls decorated by windows and balconies, in much the same manner as are the exterior facades of palaces. The audience finds itself on a piazza taking an evening *passeggiata* as it were, playing their roles and thus being included in the action. In several medieval cities the public spaces are transformed into theatres in the summertime, whereby a stage is set up, the city itself serving as a backdrop. It is usually the historical buildings that become part of this because of their artificial night illumination, although everybody recognises them as integral parts of the cityscape. A play between illusion and reality is created. As Shakespeare says: 'All the world's a stage – and all the men and women merely players: they have their exits and their entrances.'[104] The theatre becomes a mirror of the world, of interior and exterior, stage and auditorium whereby actor and audience take up a dialogue with each other.

✳

Rossi's undogmatic, complex world view is made apparent in the design for the Museum of German History in Berlin (1988; illustration on p202), which now will not even be commenced, although it stood at the centre of strong controversies for many years. After the unification of Germany, it was decided to relocate the museum, for which the new building in the western part of the city had been planned,[105] to a building in the eastern part of town, that had served as a museum for a long period of time. Rossi's design can be counted among his most important projects. He himself writes in an explanatory report for the competition: 'Does our project wish to provide a picture of German history? No, this is surely impossible from today's point of view. The possibility for synthesis is broken at the present time, we can at the most provide fragments: fragments of life, fragments of history and fragments of buildings. Intelligent architecture today attempts to bring together these fragments, after rejecting Romanticism and the closely related ideas of nihilism. It wishes to encourage a universal concept which anyone can follow by judging it according to his own standards.'[106] It was clear to Rossi that only a complex of richly structured, miscellaneous buildings and not huge, monolithic architecture could pay justice to the demands. One could describe the building area enclosed by two roads as a right-angled triangle where the hypotenuse is formed by the River Spree. The actual museum follows this direction, whereby the three-storey exhibition buildings with their steep, gabled windows are set up in a row[107]. The visitor enters the complex through a mighty rotunda that connects the museum building to the activity centre. Both buildings and their entrances face a frontal public space, following along a street bordering onto the *Tiergarten*, a large landscaped park. The elongated administrative building with its colonnade juts out to meet this street here and then follows it at right angles. The back side, along with the exhibition space, encloses a triangular courtyard in which is found a large oak. Finally, a tower can be found on the side facing the water. The design for this history museum reflects the concept of the northern city in a perhaps purer manner than would have been possible with a German architect – the idea of a northern city, marked by contrasts, just like past and present, and yet forming a unity.

It is significant that the design is not symmetrical, as is usually the case with Rossi. It is more of an ensemble that carries with it numerous associations, without suggesting a final solution. Therefore, column-/colonnade-house and oak form a contrasting pair (Italy – longing for the antique and nature mysticism) and both face the buildings influenced by industrial architecture. With its strictly rational architectural language, this contrasts with the gables of the exhibition hall. The entrance rotunda can be seen as part of the great tradition of round buildings, referring to Schinkel's museum rotunda as a place of enlightenment. It is, at the same time, no longer a place of holy mise-en-scène. In the foreword of a publication about the museum, Rossi writes of the efforts of the many people concerned with the building plans: 'It was a similar matter in former times when the ancient cathedrals were erected. I believe that the Berlin museum is a cathedral in this sense. I take up this appealing idea again consciously, even if it did nothing to further my case during the controversies about the museum. Cathedrals, basilicas, museums and town halls are sites of the collective memory. Which site encompasses the collective memory more strongly than a museum? To confuse the term cathedral or basilica with an abstract monumentalism is ignorant or misleading. It is certain, that faced by either the "art clinics", or an architectural overlapping of art and history, we prefer to stroll through the large halls of the Prado, or the wonderful rooms filled with the monumental reconstructions of antique art in the Pergamon Museum in Berlin.' [108]

At the present time, the new Bonnefanten Museum (1990; illustration on p170) is being constructed as the symbolic centre of a large new building programme in the old ceramic quarter of Maastricht, which is outside the old city. It includes a new city administrative building and 160 residential houses.

Manfredo Tafuri and Francesco Dal Co, in a book on contemporary architecture published in 1978, write that: 'It is solely in the work of the Italian, Aldo Rossi, that one can find the programmatic search for a site in which form can regain a language of forms. Rossi has the following in common with Louis Kahn: the will to depict a longing. Rossi's architecture takes note of the disappearance of logical order in the makings of architecture, which has collapsed as a result of the self-assertiveness of the bourgeois world. He does not, however, grieve over a situation preceding these changes but longs for a formal language reaching back to its origins. Rossi, like Kahn, fights against the "loss of the golden mean" but does not hope for outside help. Logic can only assert itself to the degree in which formal language is created from a constantly changing mode of expression whose original semantic value remains intact.' [109] On a coloured sketch of the Maastricht Museum, Rossi has included an aphorism, as is often the case, this time in German, *Loss of the Golden Mean* (*Verlust der Mitte*; illustration on p172). This surely refers both to the Tafuri and Dal Co text, as well as to the highly controversial programmatic post-war book by Hans Sedlmayr. The German art historian makes a plea for the upkeep of moral, ethical and above all religious values by means of art. [110] Rossi was familiar with this author. In 1958, he had written an article entitled *Criticism we Reject* [111] reviewing Sedlmayr's book, *The Revolution of Modern Art*, published in Italian in the same year. He refers extensively to the work *Loss of the Golden Mean*, denouncing the reactionary ideology of the author as being unacceptable. His main concern is with Sedlmayr's rejection of large sections of modern art. As Rossi was working with a collection of modern art in the case of the Bonnefanten Museum, the quotation on the drawing points to the fact that the post-war debate on modern art, a discussion particular to Germany, has long since been accepted as an historical phenomenon. At the same time, it raises questions in an otherwise colourful, rather joyful drawing that are applicable to any time.

The museum complex with its symmetrical, E-shaped ground plan has an entrance on the side of the enclosed body of the building. The high, centred wing frames the huge portal, reminiscent of industrial buildings. This protruding, brick wing stands out against the light, stuccoed window wall, as do the windowless side wings. The visitor enters a foyer that is, in turn, lit by a light well running through all storeys. It becomes narrower from floor to floor like a telescope. In the middle, vertical wing one finds a long, high hall of stairs that receives light from a glass roof. This long flight of steps refers to Holland, in Rossi's opinion, as well as to the northern world (*mondo gotico*) of 'Shakespearean taverns, like the unsteady Konrad and all the other shipwrecked northern figures on the seas of the south. We have attempted to show the geometric kernel of this world, while being fully aware of the fact that one can only be shipwrecked by reaching beyond geometry.'[112] The entire complex is dominated by a huge, round tower that lies at the end of the middle wing and therefore exactly opposite the main entrance. It is flanked by two, narrow stair towers over which the visitor reaches an observation platform. Having reached this, one can walk around the spire of the tower and look over the roofs of the museum.

Rossi was fascinated by the idea of constructing a museum for contemporary art on a remote site of natural beauty, as was the case with the small museum of Vassivière (1988; illustration on p146). He chooses forms of architecture that could again be read as carriers of meaning with ironic undertones. A tower once more plays an important role, a 'lighthouse' that sends its metaphorical signal into the distance (Rossi himself writes that the lighthouse has always been a psychological and architectural obsession of his). It serves as an observation tower. The actual exhibition space is an elongated section, covered by local granite. It has semicircular arcades running below the roof moulding, reminiscent of an aqueduct. The complex is highly differentiated from its surroundings. It is these surroundings that are transformed into the actual cultural landscape – like the buildings of a landscaped park that reflect our modern relationship with nature in a particularly significant manner.

In many discussions about urban planning and also in the course of planning schools and universities, Rossi assigns special importance to libraries. For this reason, as well as because of its important position in his oeuvre, one should mention the design for the Landesbibliothek Karlsruhe (1979; illustration on p190) that was never completed. The buildings of the library join a central glass gallery dominating the whole. This can be seen in several projects from then on, above all in the Museum of German History. A portico flanked by a colonnade is designed to face the street, in order to form a contrast to a Palladian church by Friedrich Weinbrenner. Several other buildings close the complex off from the neighbouring streets. Rossi has succeeded in creating a design that forms a link between an impressive architectural entity and its surroundings in a sensitive manner.

One must consider the Seregno library (1989; illustration on p176) as another important project, particularly due to Rossi's theoretical ideas on the subject. The spiritual/conceptual (*geistig*) historical example underlying the plans is the famous design for a library created by Boullée in 1785, where a huge hall has walls with bookshelves, running along several floors, that are accessible to anyone from the upper floors of the galleries.[113] Above this, a colonnade carries a barrel vaulted roof. The visitors are portrayed discussing in groups, writing or sunk in thought. Boullée writes that he was referring to Raphael's School of Athens from the *stanze* of the Vatican[114]. Philosophers and ancient sages of antiquity are gathered together in a huge hall reminiscent of Constantine's Basilica and the extension of the Dome of St Peter's, several of them discussing together in a group, while the others are silent. Many of the figures depicted can be recognised as resembling contemporary artists eg Heraclitius looks like Michelangelo, Euclid like Bramante. One also encounters members of the Gonzaga and Della Rovere families. Plato and Aristotle are depicted at the centre of the action. Plato, whose face resembles that of Leonardo da Vinci, holds his book *Timaios* in one hand. His right hand held vertically points towards heaven as the origin of all ideas. Aristotle carries the *Ethics* in his left hand. His right arm, with the open hand pointing in front horizontally, embodies the idea of a positive spirit. In one of his sketches for the Seregno library (illustration on p176), Rossi refers to Boullée, allowing the figures of Plato and Aristotle to appear behind the design. He entitles the drawing *Scuola d'Atene*. He writes that a modern library should make use of highly developed systems of systematisation, computers and videos. Beyond this, however, he links the library to a cultural vision in which it becomes a place for research and spirituality where both old and young can enter into discussions. It is a truly democratic place where everyone can gain access to the knowledge of past and present. This can only be made possible if governed by a central idea, namely that which in Raphael's design allows for *concordia*, the harmony of diverging points of view 'and which could also be our motto'.[115] Here, once again, as with the University of Miami or in the design for the Museum of German History in Berlin, a rotunda creates the entrance foyer. He assigns an important role to this hall, that is the first one to be seen by the visitor: 'In architecture, just as in the life of man and in his relationships, the beginning is just as important as the end'.[116] One should point out a connection with a Milanese church, San Nazaro Maggiore, which is one of the eleven main churches of Milan founded by St Ambrose. Bramantino built the burial chapel of Count Trivulzio in 1512-18 (illustration on p69). This is to be found at the side of the entrance, superimposed on a medieval, centrally planned building. The visitor who has just left behind him the liveliness of the Corso di Porta Romana finds himself in a huge, quiet rotunda, making him forget the everyday in one fell swoop. It is only after this that he reaches the Romanesque/Gothic part of the building, a site of religious life with its frescoes and altars. A central research and reading room, reminiscent of Boullée, follows on from the rotunda, leading on to a third complex of buildings with offices, assembly rooms and a cafeteria that surround an inner, quadratic courtyard. Again, as is the case with many of the other symmetrical buildings (*Baukörper*), one is reminded of the aforementioned drawing in which Rossi connects the ground plans of

Milan, San Nazaro Maggiore, interior of the Trivulzio Chapel
by Bartolomeo Suardi (Bramantino), 1512-18

the cemetery of Modena and the school at Fagnano Olona with the skeleton of a fish.

During the course of designing the Church of San Carlo alla Barona (1990; illustration on p174) for the Milan suburb Cascina Bianca, Rossi was conscious of the fact that it was important to provide a relatively insignificant peripheral area with an impressive centre. He also realised that it was his task to construct the spatial programme for a religious community but also to find an architectural form that could be understood as a visual expression of the church, the church that has up until the present day embodied the historical and cultural identity in Italy. He is highly convinced of the fact that nothing really innovative can take place in church architecture. The church itself signifies tradition and one should create a building appropriate for today that is a typological reference to tradition. He writes: 'It is certain that our forefathers had a natural relationship with the church and that the order of the church corresponded to that of architecture ... In this way all churches were beautiful and it made little difference if the architect was unimaginative or crazy.'[117] Several great master builders may have greatly added to the significance held by the church, and yet San Fidele in Milan or the Sacri Monti were above all created by Bishop Carlo Borromeo, and only in second place by his architect. 'The devotional buildings experienced the miserable demise of bourgeois architecture during modernism.'[118] Along with his colleagues, Rossi aimed to express the spiritual idea of the church by means of architectural forms. 'We therefore hope to construct a church that is to be large, beautiful and, above all, able to bring order to disorder, as was the case with San Carlo, whose name it carries.'[119] These remarks should not, however, be taken to mean that contrary to earlier remarks he simply identifies function with the form of a building or single architectural forms with symbolic content. In the *Scientific Autobiography* he writes: '... It is similar to the concept of the sacred in architecture. A tower is neither a religious symbol, nor one of power.'[120] It is only by coming into use, that form and content enter a symbiosis while still being able to undergo changes in the course of time, as has been stated elsewhere. In this way the facade, that is related to Rossi's secular building in many basic ways, is of paramount importance: it becomes the image of the church, an element of the liturgy made visible. Its ground floor consists of huge granite flagstones, with brick walls above it and it is structured by four huge towers in front of one wall. Two terracotta mouldings divide these into three floors. Towards the right and left, between the towers, in front of the upper, highly jutting out storey, one can find the sculptures depicting San Carlo Borromeo, the patron saint of the church, as well as of Ambrogio,[121] the patron saint of the city. The use of sculpture in building, rejected from the beginnings of modernism onwards and only taken up again by several architects in the past fifteen years, is unusual for Rossi.[122] It is necessary in this project because of the great effect that works of art, similar to that of music, have on the attitude of the congregation's response to the church service. Rossi therefore stresses his belief that it is necessary to uphold collective memories in order to deal with present and future in a world flooded by images of triviality. The actual ecclesiastical space is a modest nave, decorated solely by round steel columns in front of the outer walls, carrying the open ceiling rafters. Light enters through prefabricated, square industrial windows, reminding one of factory buildings, as do the outer walls decorated simply by pre-varnished tin. The simplicity of all the building materials is meant to remind one of the early Christian communities and is also reminiscent of Cistercian monasteries, where all elements used to build praying, living and farming structures were exactly the same. The church and the one-storey community centre form a square, monastery courtyard, surrounded by a cloister. In the middle of this lies an area surrounded by a lattice fence in which one finds a cross on a stone plinth. This church square plays an important role in community life, as it is partially open to the public. The tower rising up next to the church comprises the third section of the complex and stands wholly in the tradition of the free-standing, Italian *campanile*. In this design, Rossi has forged a link between modern community life and the respectful awe of tradition.

✽

In order to understand Rossi, one must take into account the extent to which his roots lie in the Catholic world of his Lombard home. This would actually seem to be one of the main requirements for an understanding of his work and has long been overlooked abroad. Drawings again and again lead one back to these origins. In many of them, it is the body or simply the hand of San Carlone, one of the aforementioned, large statues on Lake Maggiore, that is made visible. In his *Scientific Autobiography*,[123] Rossi describes his fascination for the Sacri Monti[124] that has continued since his childhood. These are mountains on which chapels have been densely erected according to a strict plan, in which one finds life-sized terracotta figures depicting naturalistic scenes from the life of Christ or of the saints. It is important to note that for him 'the story of deliverance found in the plaster figure, in the unmistakable gesture, in the expression frozen in time is transferred completely to the present – as a story that cannot be told in another manner.'[125] When he later came to know Edward Hopper's paintings[126] in New York, they 'lead' him 'back to the unchangeable, unchanging, timeless magical objects – tables that remain permanently laid, drinks that are never drunk, things that exist simply in their own right.'[127] The pictorial world of religion remains alive in Italy up until the present day, and Rossi refers to it by, for example, sticking small pictures of the saints, these visible signs of popular religious belief, on several of his own drawings. Here, one can sense the longing of modern man for the unshakable religiosity of simpler folks, as is the case in Pasolini's Teorema,[128] where it is only the peasant housekeeper Emilia who is able to love unselfishly and who is finally sanctified. In the catalogue accompanying the exhibition *Architetture Padane*,[129] Rossi refers to himself as 'ambrosian' (*ed io ambrosiano*), in order to differentiate himself from Luigi Ghirri from Modena and Giovanni Jacometti from Novara. By describing Milan as the city of St Ambrose, he, on the one hand, expresses his love of its great past clearly and, on the other, also demonstrates his belief in the existence of a spiritual force underlying the historical picture of the city that cannot be reached at solely a simple analysis of facts and is inextricably linked to the great ecclesiastical teacher of the fourth century. In many of his reflections, Rossi describes one of his key experiences as being a feeling for time in which his own life and doings are but momentary/fleeting. He becomes a historian who is already observing the present and therefore also his work from a distance: 'It seems as if things re-occur with the continuity of myth, and that we are therefore always in the process of translating an antique drawing.'[130]

Rossi's roots in tradition are therefore closely connected to his relationship to Lombardy, and in particular to Milan and the north Italian lakes. The area's architecture and its cities with their medieval bourgeois/middle-class culture had a highly intensive effect on him and this is the key experience underlying his work. In the same way, Renaissance painters created idealised cityscapes and architectural visions in order to contrast reality with elements that could be blended in to an embodiment of culture and spirituality. Rossi writes that, despite all his doubts, he believes in a 'great civic (*civile*) architecture that is capable of bringing the city back together, allowing us to live in a place that has greater freedom, justice and beauty.'[131] By carrying his abilities out into the world he stands in the tradition of the itinerant master builders of the north Italian lakes, who travelled over areas reaching from Sicily to St Petersburg.

View of an ideal city, tempera on wood, second half of the 15th century,
Urbino, Galleria delle Marche

Notes

1 Aldo Rossi, 'Frammenti', in: *Aldo Rossi, Architetture 1959-87*, Ed Alberto Ferlenga, Milan, 1987 (abbreviated to *Arch 1959-87* in following text), p7, (this, along with all other quotations from the texts, was originally written in Italian and translated by the author).

2 Aldo Rossi, *L' Architettura della Città*, in: Biblioteca di Architettura e Urbanistica, vol 8, Padua, 1966; Germ ed: *Die Architektur der Stadt*, in: Bauwelt Fundamente 41, ed Ulrich Conrads, Düsseldorf, 1973 (abbreviated to *Arch d St* in the following).

3 ibid, p12.

4 ibid, p28.

5 ibid, p28.

6 ibid, p45.

7 ibid, p45.

8 ibid, conclusion of the German edition, p174.

9 ibid, p104.

10 Aldo Rossi, 'Design for Planning an Area on the Banks of the Connecting Canal, 1976', in: Heinrich Klotz, *Moderne und Postmoderne*, Braunschweig/Wiesbaden, 1987 (abbreviated to H Klotz in following text), p252.

11 Quatremère de Quincy (1755-1849), *Dictionnaire Historique de L'Architecture*, 3 vols Paris 1795-1825, 1832[2].

12 Quatremère de Quincy, quoted from *Arch d St* op cit, p27.

13 ibid, p28.

14 ibid.

15 *Wissenschaftliche Selbstbiographie* (Scientific Autobiography), translated from the Italian by Heinrich Helfenstein, Bern-Berlin, 1988 (English edition, Cambridge, Massachusetts,

1981. Abbreviated to *Wiss Selbstb* in following text), p9.

16 'La Città Analoga', 1976; here quoted from: *Aldo Rossi, Arch 1959-87*, op cit, p118. In the Spanish edition of *L'Arquitectura Analoga* (in: 'Construcción de la Ciudad') Rossi quotes a letter by CG Jung (dated 2nd March, 1910) in which he writes that logical thought is similar to thinking aloud in words, and that analogical thinking is archaic, subconscious and practically impossible to express in language.

17 ibid.

18 In a description of the rebuilding and extension of the Hotel Duca, Milan, 1988 (photo on p158), Rossi refers to the blind windows on the back facade with the remark that *é molto importante per il decoro urbano*; quoted from: *Aldo Rossi, Architetture 1988-1992*, ed Alberto Ferlenga, Milan, 1992 (abbreviated as *Arch 1988-92* in following text), p140. Concerning the ideal of beauty in the Italian city, compare: Wolfgang Braunfels, Mittelalterliche Stadtbaukunst in der Toskana, Berlin, 1953, 1982[5], p126 f.

19 Aldo Rossi, *Architetture Padane*, catalogue of the exhibition in the Casa del Mantegna, Mantua, 1984 (abbreviated to *Arch Pad* in following text).

20 Andrea Mantegna (1431-1506). *Death of the Madonna*, about 1460, height: 54cm, width: 42 cm, Madrid, Museo del Prado.

21 *Ach Pad*, op cit, p12.

22 *Wiss Selbstb*, op cit, p92.

23 *Arch 1959-87*, op cit, p41.

24 In the projects by Rossi discussed in the following, the year of the design is cited, while the length of the construction period is only given in exceptional cases.

25 *Arch 1959-87*, op cit, p33.

26 Marc-Antoine Laugier, *Essai sur L'Architecture*, Paris, 1753; modern edition: ibid 1953 (new German edition: M-A Laugier, *Das Manifest des Klassizismus*, Zürich/München, 1989).

27 ibid, p35.

28 Peter Eisenman (born 1932), 'The House of the Dead as the City of Survival', in: *Aldo Rossi in America: 1976-1979*, catalogue of the exhibition of the Institute for Architecture and Urban Studies, New York, 1979, pp14-15.

29 One should take particular note of the similarities to simple, Etruscan 'aedicula' graves.

30 *Wiss Selbstb*, op cit, pp12-14.

31 H Klotz, op cit, p244.

32 *Wiss Selbstb*, op cit, p20.

33 In his *Manifesto of the Architecture of Futurism* (name invented by FT Marinetti) dating from 1914, Antonio Sant'Elia damns the entire canon of Classical architecture and all forms of decoration are rejected. Many architects believed that they could help significantly in bringing about a better, more just society. In this vein, Bruno Taut writes, in 1920, in the series of visionary essays entitled *The Glass Chain*, put together by himself and Adolf Behne: 'Our dawn glows in the distance. Hurrah, three times hurrah for our kingdom without violence. Hurrah for all that one can see through, that is clear! Hurrah for purity! Hurrah for the crystalline! And hurrah and evermore hurrah for all that flows, is graceful, spiky, sparkling, that is like lightening, that is light - hurrah for eternal building!' Quoted from: 'Programme und Manifeste zur Architektur des 20. Jahrhunderts', *Bauwelt Fundamente*, vol 1, ed Ulrich Conrads, Berlin, 1964, p54.

34 Museum of German History, Berlin, *Aldo Rossis Entwurf im Gefüge der Kulturforen*, ed. Alberto Ferlenga, Stuttgart, 1991 (first Italian edition, Milan, 1990), p16.

35 Giorgio Grassi (born 1937). 'Der Formalismus in der modernen Architektur', in: *Freibeuter* 12, 1982, p87; and he goes on to add: 'Much has been said about so-called "Pillar Architecture". Modern criticism has identified pillars found in contemporary architecture with fascist dictatorships and has therefore behaved in much the same farcical manner as did the dictatorships themselves.'

36 *Arch d St*, op cit, p94.

37 *Architettura Razionale*, XV Triennale di Milano, Sezione Internazionale de Architettura, Milan, 1973, p69; Rossi's theory of rationalism was highly influential in Italy and countless pupils and followers now follow his example. One should make particular mention of Rossi's Milanese colleague, Giorgio Grassi, who has played a large role in the founding of rationalism (*Architettura Razionale*).

38 *Arch d St*, op cit, p28.

39 The incomplete design was created with Giorgio Grassi.

40 are also with H Klotz, op cit, p258.

41 Andrea Palladio (1508-80), Villa Sarego, *c*1569, in St Sofia di Pedemonte, Verona.

42 'Aspetti dell'Architettura tedesca contemporanea', in: *Casabella Continuità* no 235, 1960. Here Rossi also compares the buildings on the Stalinallee (that he calls a 'Muscovite suburb' and considers problematic in the Berlin context) with the Interbau (Hansaviertel) buildings – these he considers justifiable examples of a modernity attempting to create a cosmopolitan city.

43 'Aspetti della tipologia residenziale a Berlino', in: *Casabella Continuità* no 288, 1964. Rossi writes at length about various types of houses, referring in particular to tenement buildings and housing estates. He then concentrates on the Hansa area (Hansaviertel) which he regards as a problematic example of the reconstruction of a central area (although several buildings can be regarded as a success), as it has not been successfully incorporated into the historical part of the city. He describes the Stalinallee as a cultural borderline case where the role residential buildings should play was not worked out beforehand. Despite this, however, he adds that it is an impressive piece of urban planning (*urbanistischer Eingriff*) and should be judged from this point of view.

44 *Architettura Razionale*, XV Triennale di Milano, op cit; the essay, 'Architettura per i centri storici', by Ezio Bonifanti, also discusses the Stalinallee (Karl-Marx-Allee). It is described as one of the positive aspects of the reconstruction of the destroyed city. In his introduction, Rossi also defends the Karl-Marx-Allee, as well as several buildings in Moscow. He calls it an important example of urban planning where questions of style become superfluous.

45 Compare with Alberto Ferlenga, 'Die rote deutsche Kathedrale', in: *Deutsches Historisches Museum, Berlin, Aldo Rossi's Entwurf im Gefüge der Kulturforen,* op cit, p9 ff.

46 The standard height for eaves in Berlin is 22 metres, which became legally binding in the nineteenth century.

47 Aldo Rossi, 'Berliner Schützenstrasse', unpublished text, December, 1992.

48 *Arch 1959-87*, op cit, p54.

49 Rossi mentions the *tomba del fornaio* twice in the text. He is referring to the Roman tomb of the baker and redeemer, Eurysace, found in front of the Porta Maggiore and dating from the second quarter of the first century BC. This proud tradesman wished to prosaically celebrate his work in the monumental travertine structure, rather than achieve an artistic effect. Therefore, one finds here a replica of a technical system with its vertical and horizontal tubes, used to measure the grain. A realistic frieze depicts the making of

bread in a rather sober manner. Rossi was obviously fascinated by this job-oriented tomb where life has been frozen into timelessness.

50 *Arch 1959-87*, op cit, p54.
51 ibid.
52 *Wiss Selbsth*, op cit, p78.
53 *Arch d St,* op cit, p94.
54 Compare also H Klotz, op cit, p251.
55 In 1981, Rossi published the *Studies on Palladian Elements (Doric order)* by Christopher Stead, which could be the inspiration for his burial chapel, in: Architettura/Idea, catalogue of the XVI Triennale di Milano, ed. Aldo Rossi, Luca Meda, Daniele Vitale, Florence, 1981, p84.
56 ibid, p16.
57 *Arch 1959-87*, op cit, p41.
58 ibid; he could be referring to Schinkel's watercolour and pencil drawing of the ground plan of an antique country house for the Crown Prince at Charlottenhof (1833). (Schinkel Collection, Collection of the State Museums of Berlin, SM 34.27.)
59 Gajus Caecilius Secundus Plinius (61-62 AD in Como! – 114). Architects have referred to the two ideal prototypes of villas, Tusca and Laurentia, since the Renaissance.
60 *Arch 1959-87*, op cit, p98.
61 H Klotz, op cit, pp254-255.
62 ibid, p256.
63 The Italian word *pasta* refers to several types of farinaceous foodstuffs.
64 Rossi's first incorporation of an old factory chimney is in the construction of the school at Fagnano Olona in 1972.
65 *Arch 1959-87*, op cit, p200.
66 Santa Maria della Presentazione, referred to as *delle Zitelle*, has a simple, Palladian facade. Rossi referred to this facade in his design for the *Teatro del Mondo* (1979). In 1982, he developed a restoration project for the monastery complex, so that it could be made use of by the university.
67 The Venetian words for public space, street and alley are *campo, calle* and *vicolo,* repectively.
68 *Arch 1988-92*, op cit, p224.
69 Claude-Nicolas Ledoux (1736-1806), Etienne-Louis Boullée (1728-99); Rossi translated Boullée's *Treatise on Architecture* into Italian and wrote an introduction to it: *Etienne-Louis Boullée, Architettura. Saggio sull'arte*, Padua, 1967; in the explanatory report concerning the Congress Centre in Milan (1982), he himself mentions Boullée in reference to the conical tower, in: *Arch 1959-87*, op cit, p212.
70 A circular hall is found, for example, in the designs for the University of Miami (1986) and in those for the administrative building of the UBS/SBG (1990).
71 *Arch 1988-92*, op cit, p214.
72 ibid.
73 The interview was held by Nicola di Battista and Vittorio Magnano Lampugnani on June 20th, 1990, in Berlin; printed in: *Domus*, no 722, 18.12. 1990.
74 *Arch 1988-92*, op cit, p214.
75 The name refers to the ink pen company, Aurora, that could formerly be found on this site.
76 Gruppo Finanzario Tessile.

77 Turin has been the capital city of the House of Savoy since the Middle Ages. This has been the main influence on the city up until the present day.

78 Surrounded by the cathedral, camposanto, baptistry and the former Ospedale di Santa Chiara, the buildings are connected to each other by a grass area.

79 *Arch 1988-92*, op cit, p284.

80 The Dogana da Mar is the old tax station at the exit of the Canal Grande into the Canale di S Marco. It is a picturesque, seventeenth-century tower building. On it, the statue of Fortuna stands on a globe carried by two Atlas figures and turns in the wind.

81 Formerly Lenin-Allee.

82 *Arch 1988-92*, op cit, p94.

83 ibid, p158.

84 ibid, p176.

85 ibid, p74. The term 'demon of analogy' may also refer to Daniel Libeskind, who used this term in a discussion about the Teatro del Mondo – Rossi qotes the term in an essay. in: *Arch 1959-87*, op cit, p154.

86 The posthumously published novel *Petrolio* by Pier Paolo Pasolini is filmed in a fragmentary style. In reference to the only partially extant Roman novel, *Satyricon* by Petronius, completed segments alternate with summaries of the missing parts, in the manner of the historical-critical edition of this fragmentary text. Documentary material and reflections on the novel form also alternate with one another.

87 Aldo Rossi, 'Frammenti', in: *Arch 1959-87*, op cit, p7.

88 In the catalogue to the exhibition 'Architetture Padane', op cit, p13, Rossi writes that the studies with the skeleton of a horse refer to the book *The Anatomy of the Horse* by George Stubbs. These horses had interested him because of the structure and form of their skeletons. He contrasts his own drawings with the wall-paintings of horses by Rinaldo Mantovano and Benedetto Pagni (after designs by Giulio Romano) in the Scala dei Cavalli, in the Palazzo Te in Mantua. These create the illusion of creatures that have been frozen in time in the hall for centuries. They are placed in front of landscapes, suggesting views to the outside, enclosed by painted pilasters.

89 *Wiss Selbstb*, op cit, in several parts of the text; the bronze sculpture is without a base, 23.4 metres high.

90 Aldo Rossi, 'Il nome', in: *Casa Aurora, Un' Opera di Aldo Rossi*, ed Vittorio Savi, Turin, 1987, p41.

91 *Wiss Selbstb*, op cit, p101.

92 *Arch 1959-87*, op cit, p80.

93 The Palladio motif, where a middle arch is flanked by two, narrower openings, was often used by Palladio. It was probably developed by Bramante and published by Serlio in his *Architettura*. In Broni, a right-angled, main opening and two narrower and lower side openings form a unity with the windows lying above.

94 Antonio Averlino, called Filarete (*c*1400-69).

95 The added title *scientifico* (scientific) refers to the scientific theatre in Mantua, the anatomical theatre in Padua and other smaller, above all Italian, theatres of the eighteenth century.

96 *Arch 1959-87*, op cit, p128.

97 Manfredo Tafuri, 'Il 'caso' Aldo Rossi', in: Manfredo Tafuri, *Storia dell'Architettura Italiana 1944-1985*, Turin, 1982; 1986[2], p169.

98 *Wiss Selbstb*, op cit, p46.

99 In 1986, Rossi designed the stage designs for *Lucia di Lammamoor* and *Madame Butterfly*, for the open-air stage in the Rocca Brancaleone in Ravenna, for performances by the Teatro Communale of Bologna; in 1992, he designed the stage set and costumes for *Elektra* (illustration on p186) at the Greek theatre in Taormina.

100 Carlo Francesco Barabino (1768-1835). The theatre in Genoa was finished in 1828 after decades of in-fighting.

101 Rossi writes: 'No-one is more ready to change, destroy or refuse to reconstruct historical buildings; the future of the city is much more complex than the possibility of having just any modern building in the city centre.' in: *Arch 1959-87*, op cit, p225.

102 A competition for reconstruction had taken place in 1949, won by Paolo Chessa. The plans, however, were strictly rejected by the ministry. The local government gave the commission to Carlo Scarpa who presented a highly controversial design in 1969. In 1978, shortly before his death, he presented a second design. In 1981, a new, two-stage competition took place where Rossi emerged as the winner.

103 Rossi writes on this matter: 'In reality, the architecture of this theatre is neither modern, nor postmodern; it is simply architecture.' He adds that it is a question of technology, rather than of architecture, that determines modernity. Ibid.

104 William Shakespeare, *As You Like It*; Act II, Scene VII.

105 The Museum of German History (*Deutsches Historisches Museum*) has been housed in the Zeughaus since the unification of Germany. This is a building, dating from c1700, that largely stems from Andreas Schlüter.

106 Text accompanying the competition for the Museum of German History, in: *Deutsches Historisches Museum, Berlin, Aldo Rossi's Entwurf im Gefüge der Kulturforen*, op cit, p40.

107 Rossi also envisaged steep roofs in his first German museum design, for Marburg, 1987 (illustration on p192). The two-storey buildings, in a grass area near the River Lahn, form an inner courtyard which includes a sculpture by Georg Kolbe.

108 *Deutsches Historisches Museum*, Berlin, Aldo Rossi's Entwurf im Gefüge der Kulturforen, op cit, p7; in the explanatory report for his competition entry (1988), Rossi states that he is against 'reducing the museum to a clinic for history and art, a unity comprising white, antiseptic walls, windows, repeated and repeating galleries, that take it in turns to house this or that piece of history (or art or ethnology). They are like good, antiseptic and efficient hospitals, well equipped to take in a patient. They even tend to abstract from his status as patient, turning him into a clinical case, whether it be in Texas or Frankfurt am Main.'

109 Manfredo Tafuri, Francesco Dal Co, Gegenwart, in: *Weltgeschichte der Architektur*, Stuttgart, 1988 (Italian first edition: Milan, 1978), p219.

110 Hans Sedlmayr, *Verlust der Mitte, Die bildende Kunst des 19 und 20 Jahrhunderts als Symbol der Zeit*, Salzburg, 1948.

111 Aldo Rossi, 'Una critica che respingiamo', in: *Casabella Continuità* no 219.

112 *Arch 1988-92*, op cit, p258.

113 In 1981, Rossi refers to Boullée and to Raphael's *School of Athens*, in the article entitled 'Architettura/Idea', in: *Architettura/Idea*, catalogue of the XVI Triennale di Milano, op cit, p15.

114 Raphael (1483-1520) arrived in Rome in 1508, in order to paint the rooms of Pope Julius II. *The School of Athens* belongs to the first of the halls of the Stanze della Segnatura, dating from 1508-11.

115 *Arch 1988-92*, op cit, p183.

116 ibid.

117 ibid, p208.

118 ibid.

119 ibid.

120 *Wiss Selbstb*, op cit, p132.

121 St Ambrose (*c*.340, Trier – 4. 4. 397, Milan). His name day, the 7th of February, is a holiday in Milan.

122 Compare with the comparatively early use of sculpture on the courtyard side of the housing block in the Ritterstrasse in Berlin, by Rob Krier (1978-81). This form of enriching architecture by means of artistic fictions is, however, alien to Rossi.

123 *Wiss Selbstb*, op cit.

124 The *Sacri Monti* were originally erected during the Counter-Reformation as the visual expression of the renewal of faith and also of the power of the Church. They attempted to provide an alternative to the Protestanism of the north which relied heavily on the written word. They have today, however, just like the bronze sculpture depicting San Carlone, lost this meaning and have become indications of local religiosity and tradition.

125 *Wiss Selbstb*, op cit.

126 Edward Hopper (1882-1967).

127 ibid, p17.

128 Pier Paolo Pasolini, *Teorema*, Milan 1968; soon after the book was published, Pasolini reworked this material to create the film.

129 *Arch Pad*, op cit, p11.

130 Quoted from: Ada Masoero, 'Aldo Rossi, Frammenti classici e giocoso d'un mondo quasi metafisico', in: *Il Sole* 24 ore, 13. 12. 1992.

131 Aldo Rossi, *De Architettura Onesti*, 1992.

Buildings and Projects

Town Hall Public Space and Monument for the Partisans, Segrate
1965

The dominant element of the public space is the monument for the partisans. It is structured by the disposition of various architectural fragments. The public space and the monument are presented in an architecture of shadows, shadows that are pointers towards time and the passing of the seasons. One side of the monument forms a well, while the other side forms a tribune. The tribune leads to a public space that ends in a wide stairway. The outside staircase is enclosed by greenery: grass and trees.

Town Hall Public Space

Housing Block in the Gallaratese Area, Milan
1969/70

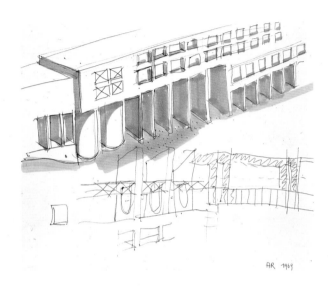

The rhythm made by the seven supports and the columns, marking the various storeys, strengthens the horizontal impression made by the building. It stands out clearly against the suburbs on the outskirts of Milan, where it has almost become an emblematic sign.

Gallaratese, Milan (and *overleaf*)

San Cataldo Cemetery, Modena
1971

The cemetery, for which there was a national competition, is surrounded by a large enclosure where one finds the graves, with a cone and a large cube in the middle. The cone is to house the chapel and the cube is for the earthly remains of those remaining in the graves (the 'zombies').

The large cemetery of Modena still plays a role in the life of this Emilian city. As perhaps the liveliest of Italian cities, its cemetery is subject to much discussion. I refer to it as the great cemetery, but in actual fact all cemeteries are great because they are the place of death.

San Cataldo Cemetery, Modena

San Cataldo Cemetery, Bone House, Modena

San Cataldo Cemetery, Modena
(and *overleaf*); in the foreground is the Jewish Cemetery

91

Primary School, Fagnano Olona
1972

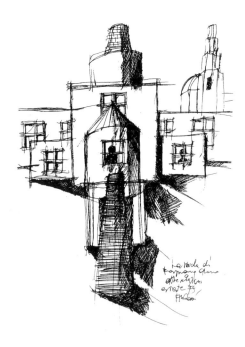

The school is marked by the closed-off courtyard. In this courtyard one finds the cylindrical library building that looks like a baptismal font. One also finds stairs that resemble a theatre with tiers. The public space is therefore also a didactic area. The children of Fagnano like their large chimney, the baptismal-font-library and private theatre very much.

Primary School, Fagnano Olona

Primary School, Fagnano Olona

Primary School, Fagnano Olona

La Città Analoga (The Analogous City)
1977

Why have I sketched the site of the city? It is because if I should speak of the architecture of today, whether it be my own or that of others, I find it important to show the connections leading from the imagination to reality and from both of these towards freedom. There are no inventions, no complexities, also no irrationality, that cannot be understood by using reason, or at least the dialectic of the concrete. I believe in the power of the imagination as a concrete possibility. The definition of the analogous city occurred to me while re-reading my book *The Architecture of the City*. In the introduction to the second edition, which I wrote several years after the book was first published, it appeared to me that description and knowledge should make way for a further area of study – the power of the imagination, arising from the concrete. It was for this reason that I concentrated on the painting by Canaletto where an imaginary Venice becomes more important than the real one, thanks to its unusual composition. This creation is made from designs and from both real and imaginary elements that are cited and brought together in order to form an alternative to reality.

The Analogous City

Secondary School, Broni
1979

The most important point of orientation is the large *aula* or central hall. This is both a geometrical and formal centre. As a pedagogical place *par excellence*, side buildings are adjacent to this. The entrance to the school is light and is reached by a straight avenue.

Secondary School, Broni

Secondary School, Broni

Secondary School, Broni

Teatro del Mondo (World Theatre), Venice
1979

This is perhaps my most famous building. It was certainly created from a feeling of both happiness and imagination. Undoubtedly, its relationship with Venice brought fortune to it. It was built of wood and iron scaffolding for the Venice Biennale and travelled to the theatre festival in Dubrovnik. Nonetheless, it was built up again for bureaucratic reasons after several years.

Teatro del Mondo, Venice (and *overleaf*)

Molteni Burial Chapel, Giussano
1980 (constructed up until 1987)

The chapel consists of two parts. One walks down a stairway leading from the grass to an underground area. Here is a hall where one finds the graves. The upper part includes a type of city gate (after a relief by Palladio on the Porta Romana in Verona), symbolising the transition from life to death. One can view the graves from this point. The whole space is lit up by the light falling from above.

Burial Chapel, Giussano

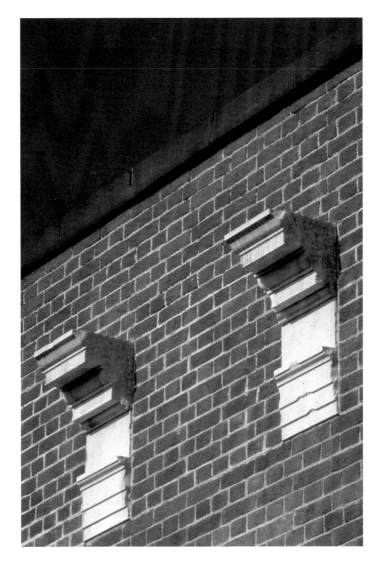

Burial Chapel, Giussano

Burial Chapel, Giussano

New Centre for the Fontivegge Area, Perugia
1982 (construction up until 1988)

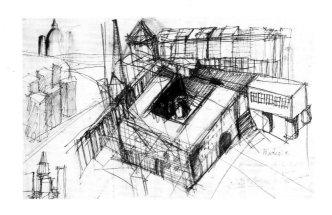

Fontivegge, Perugia

113

Fontivegge, Perugia

Fontivegge, Perugia

New Town Hall, Borgoricco
1983 (construction up until 1988)

This town hall is located in the Venetian countryside, near Padua and Venice. The reference to the Palazzo della Ragione of Padua is seen in the copper-covered, vaulted, timber roof construction and in the large area of the meeting hall.

New Town Hall, Borgoricco

New Town Hall, Borgoricco

New Town Hall, Borgoricco

Reconstruction of the Carlo Felice Theatre, Genoa
1983 (construction up until 1990)

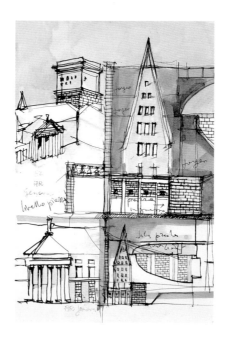

At the end wall of the Carlo Felice Theatre, parts of the old eighteenth-century Barabino building have been preserved. This is particularly obvious in the large lobby. The old theatre was partially destroyed in the war and these are the parts that have been preserved. The interior is completely new. The gridiron, containing the technology necessary for a modern theatre, is also new.

Carlo Felice Theatre, Genoa

Carlo Felice Theatre, Genoa, interior

Carlo Felice Theatre, Genoa, interior

Casa Aurora Office Building, Turin
1984 (construction up until 1987)

Turin is the most highly organised city in Italy. The GFT building has found a position between the Roman and the Savoyan areas. It is part of the new Turin, influenced by military and administrative architecture.

Casa Aurora, Turin

Casa Aurora, Turin

Casa Aurora, Turin

Centro Torri, Parma
1985 (construction until 1988)

This project is a 'happy' project. I cannot explain rationally how a certain project can be described as happy or sad. The towers are undoubtedly 'happy', stretching out to heaven. Centro Torri appears to strengthen the effect with the use of the towers, as do public buildings where the names are indicated on the end wall: 'theatre', 'town hall' etc. These names indicate their function. More importantly, however, they are fixed (*Fixpunkte*), urban points in a city that can undergo changes. The brick and ceramic towers in Parma often look like lighthouses on foggy days.

Centro Torri, Parma (and *overleaf*)

Residential Building in the Vialba Area, Milan
1985 (construction until 1990)

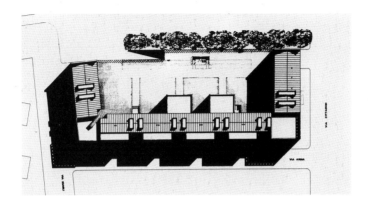

This is the largest residential house I have built in my own city. Brick and yellow stucco, traditionally Milanese colours and materials, alternate with each other.
The large corner column from Berlin is taken up again. It has, perhaps, almost become a post-Albertian symbol of architecture.

Vialba, Milan

Vialba, Milan

Vialba, Milan

Residential and Business Building in the
La Villette-Sud Area, Paris
1986 (construction until 1991)

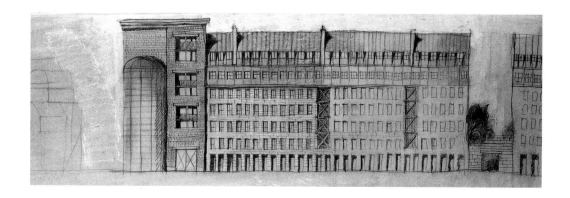

The architecture and tradition of the city, which is often progressive, is a basic subject in architecture that has always interested me. I believe that this building, with a roof that is so characteristic of Paris, above all of the Rue de Rivoli, will have a greater influence on the city than avant-garde constructions that have no relationship to the physical reality of Paris.

La Villette, Paris (and *overleaf*)

137

Il Palazzo Hotel, Fukuoka, Japan
1987 (construction up until 1989)

Il Palazzo Hotel, Fukuoka

Il Palazzo Hotel, Fukuoka

Il Palazzo Hotel, Fukuoka

Single-Family House, Mount Pocon, Pennsylvania, USA
1988/89

The architecture of this single-family house in the forests of the State of New York is similar to traditional New England architecture. I have simply made an interpretation in my quest for a personal dimension. I have always believed that it is important to develop something that already exists in my work, just as one 're-reads' a literary text.

Single-Family House, Mount Pocon

Museum for Contemporary Art, Vassivière, France
1988 (construction up until 1991)

When this project was started, elements were used that were considered appropriate for a building linked to megalithic constructions, large lakes and water.

A part of the museum is like a large lighthouse, from which one can look over the whole lake. The stone that is used is local granite, of which the statues in the interior are made.

Museum for Contemporary Art, Vassivière

Museum for Contemporary Art, Vassivière

Museum for Contemporary Art, Vassivière

Lighthouse-Theatre, Toronto, Canada
1988

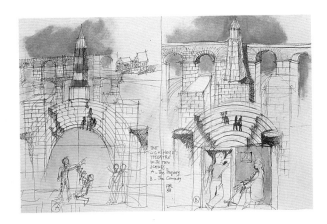

This amphitheatre on Lake Toronto refers to Roman theatres; building a bridge between Greek and modern theatre. The lighthouse, being a seafaring symbol, therefore forms a link between all analogous port cities.

Lighthouse-Theatre, Toronto

Construction of the Croce Rossa Square with
the Pertini Monument, Milan
1988 (construction until 1990)

This is designed as a small Lombard public space, as a place where one can meet, eat a sandwich or take a group photo. The Croce Rossa square is enclosed by a double row of mulberry trees and has stone benches, street lamps and a pink, granite pilaster. At the end of the public space, one finds the cube with stairs ending at a stone wall. A bronze triangle has been inserted into the wall, out of which water flows. The stone is the same reddish-grey Candoglia marble used to build Milan Cathedral. The significance of a stairway on an axis with the Via Monte Napoleone and the water is, of course, a frequent element in monuments from antique times up until the present.

Croce Rossa Square, Milan

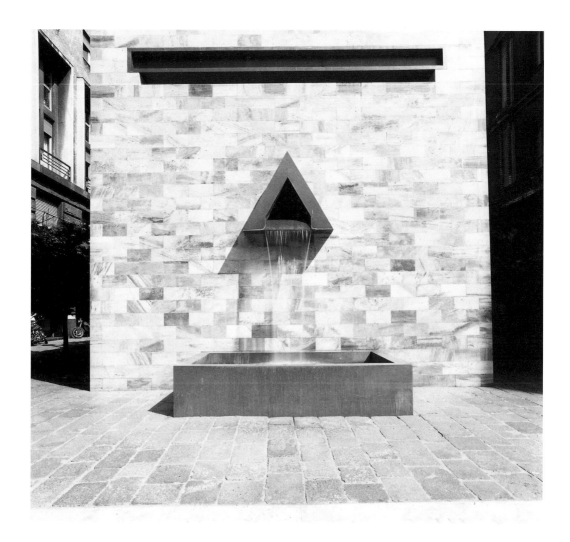

Croce Rossa Square, Milan

Croce Rossa Square, Milan

Sports Palace, Milan
1988

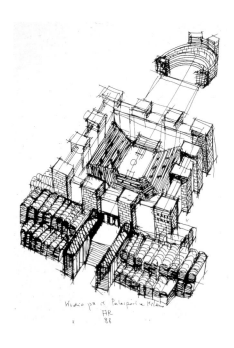

I imagined the sports palace as a large Milanese building. The design takes into account a certain idea of the city. It attempts to create a fixed point that is capable of making further developments of this idea clearer. This is both highly modern and old because it potentially takes up and foresees all possible changes. Further buildings are grouped around the sports palace, just as small shops and wretched, residential houses were squeezed up around the cathedral.

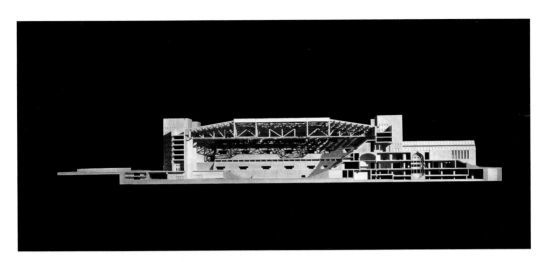

Sports Palace, Milan

Reconstruction and Extension of the Hotel Duca, Milan
1988 (construction up until 1991)

The hotel stands on the shore of a port canal and has an excellent site. It is enclosed by two streets in which there are bars and restaurants.

The compact facade is decorated by Persian red stones. Each storey is marked by a green, iron support, which gives the building its rhythm. Reminiscent of the forgotten park stones, covered by a layer of rot, a strong, mineral and plant-like green complements the red and orange, shimmering stone like furrows. This stone is that of the most ancient of kingdoms – Persia, the gateway to the Orient and mother of the Occident.

Hotel Duca, Milan

Hotel Duca, Milan

Hotel Duca, Milan

Tower with Sculpture Museum, Zandaam, The Netherlands
1989/90

The monument in Zandaam, a small town in The Netherlands, houses a small gallery. It has become a symbol and meeting-point for various activities for the inhabitants. The building is a variation on the towers that I have designed many times and that perhaps originate from those of Filarete.

Tower with Sculpture Museum, Zandaam

Casa Alessi, Verbania, Lake Maggiore
1989 (construction until 1993)

The architecture of this villa is of great interest to me because it is the first time that I was inspired by the Romantic style and could imitate this to a certain extent. Many beautiful examples of this style, that combine typically local with classical or historical elements, can be found at Lake Maggiore or Lake Como (and also in other areas of Lombardy). It is an old Valesian tradition to rough-cast the walls with granite splinters.

Casa Alessi, Verbania

Cesare Cattaneo University Building, Castellanza
1990

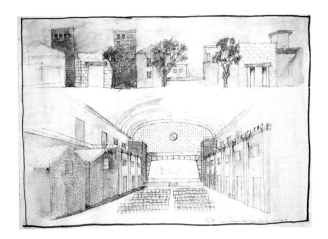

The architectural design intends to upgrade this area of the city and to link it to other urban elements, particularly taking into account the role played by the university.

The architectural interventions corresponding to the two different areas (the Corso Matteotti and the Olona Valley) and the great diversity of existing buildings is taken into account. The constructions for the administrative, secretarial and teaching buildings are planned as the central point on the Corso Matteotti. The restored Villa Jucker is envisaged for the rector. A highly significant architectural intervention is concentrated on the building in the Olona Valley in order to create space for teaching, workshops and university areas.

University Building, Castellanza
(and *overleaf*)

Bonnefanten Museum, Maastricht, The Netherlands
1990 (still under construction)

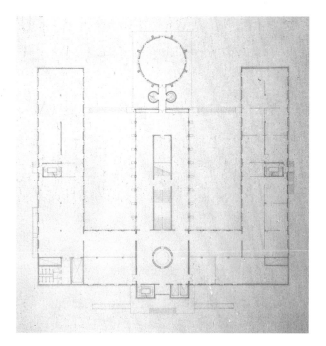

The museum rises above the further bank of the Meuse, on the opposite side to the historic city centre, lying between the large bridge still under construction and the Romanesque bridge. The building's intersection is dominated by a large stairway that links the ground storey, reaching over the entrance, with the upper storey of the dome. It is constructed of prefabricated iron-concrete parts, surrounded by stone and brick with a zinc roof on the dome.

Bonnefanten Museum, Maastricht

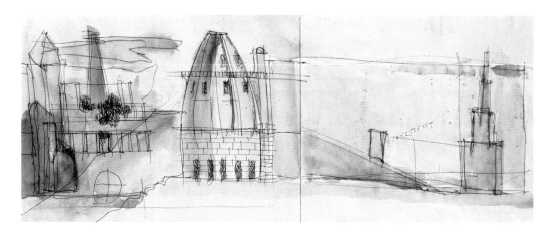

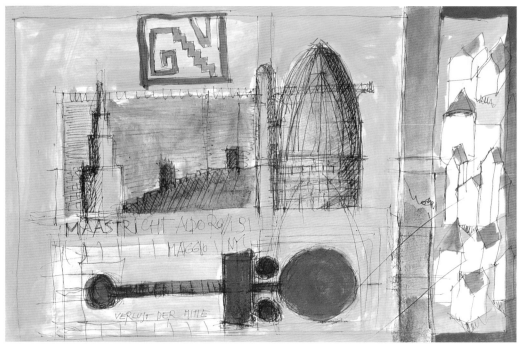

Bonnefanten Museum, Maastricht, sketch

172

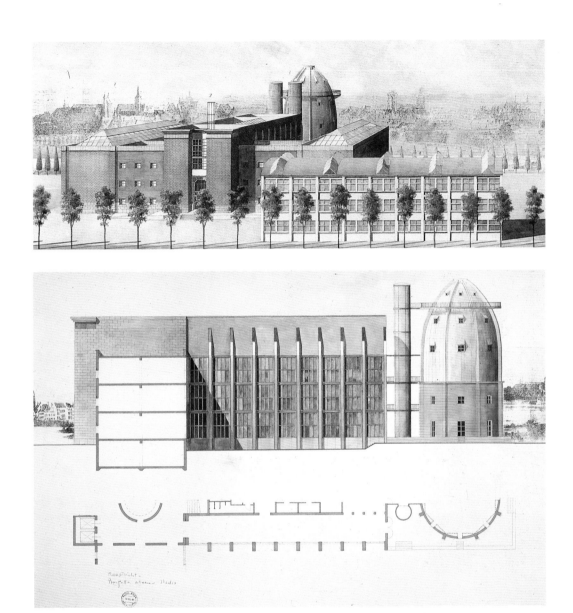

Bonnefanten Museum, Maastricht, perspective and view

173

Church of San Carlo alla Barona,
Cascina Biance Area, Milan
1990

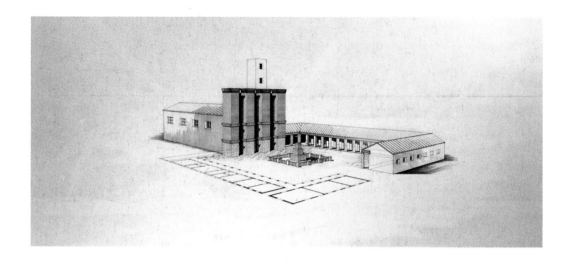

The site of this building on a corner is favourable (almost like the famous American 'corner lot'). A lasting material and timeless model were used to strengthen this ensemble character. The facade reveals bare brick in the manner of many Italian and Lombard churches that were never completed. This had various reasons, one of which was probably a certain love of the unfinished. This can be seen in eighteenth-century etchings of Milan Cathedral.

Church of San Carlo alla Barona, Milan

Library, Seregno
1990

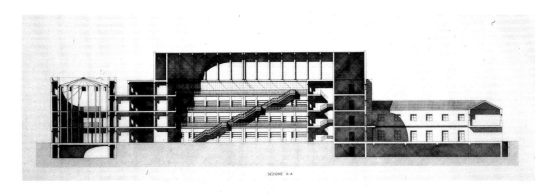

SEZIONE A-A

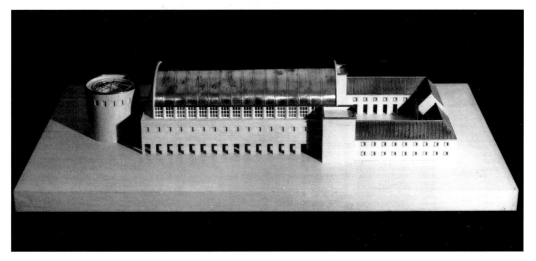

Library, Seregno

177

Congress Palace, Milan
1990

The congress palace can be seen as a part of the city that links the typology of public buildings with the courtyards and gardens of ancient Milan from the days of the Visconti and the Milan of Borromini with the senate building and priests' seminary. This tradition, partially lost in the present age, is taken up again in order to unite the green public spaces and the administrative buildings.

The palace appears like a giant 'shell'. Confused city noises of the interior are transformed into a sensible conversation, thus reversing Walter Benjamin's metaphor.

The function of cultural institutions such as universities, town halls and parliaments should be related to the above.

Congress Palace, Milan, photo of model

Linate Airport, Milan
1991 (partially still under construction)

The Linate Airport extends the airport towards the landing strips. The supporting structure includes pink granite pilasters and an entrance made of Candoglia marble. The structure made of iron supports and columns is austere in disposition and has a complex rhythm. Antique writers spoke of the sky's limits but the sky is becoming an increasingly inhabited space. Airports have therefore become the new gates of the cities and they should express their spirit and character and at the same time be ready for change.

Linate Airport, Milan (and *overleaf*)

181

AEROPORTO INTERNAZIONALE MILANO LIN.

ALDO ROSSI

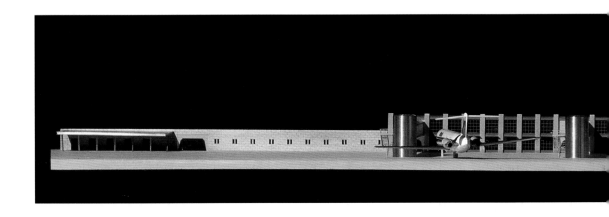

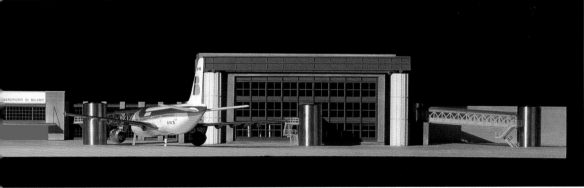

Administrative Building of the Disney Development, Orlando, Florida, USA
1991

This project is the first core of office buildings (administration, technical areas, directors' offices etc) for the Disney Company, in connection with Disney World, near Orlando, Florida. The building design and the architectural scale are inspired by the historical monuments of Pisa, above all the green space in the middle and the isolation of the buildings. The towers should attract attention in the highly monotonous landscape.

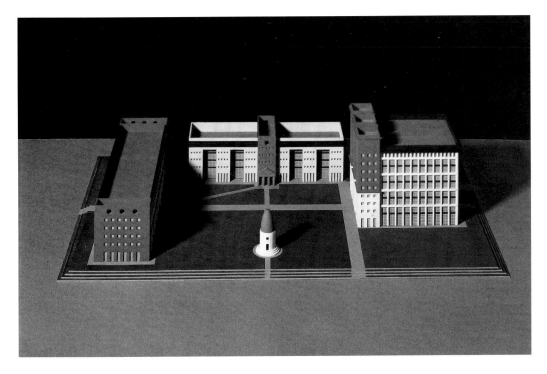

Administrative Building, Orlando, photo of model

Stage Design for *Elektra* in the Greek Theatre, Taormina
1992

I have seen this building of Atrius of our world, as we see the cities in which we live: huge ruins, derelict buildings, misery and semantic confusion (being confused by all that is said). The curse of the *House of Atrius* continues in the Los Angeles of *Blade Runner*, in the Manhattan of *Escape from New York*, in Pasolini's Rome, in both Shakespeare's London and the Docklands.

The story of the *House of Atrius* is also the story of the fall of a family, with its own madness, secret crimes or diseases.

Meaning has long since been forgotten from the large, derelict factories with their long crevices running vertically through the walls and their rusty iron machines and carriages.

Stage Design, Taormina (and *overleaf*)

County Library, Karlsruhe
1979

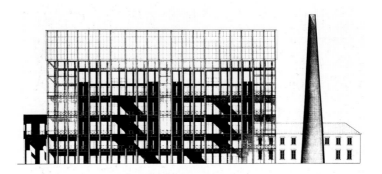

The design for the County Library follows the contours of the group of buildings by both keeping and reconstructing the old, existing buildings and also by envisaging new buildings in the interior of the complex. The en-bloc building along the street is only interrupted by the large, central gallery running through the entire ensemble of buildings. The gallery becomes a covered street, linked to both city and library. The central street is part of the historical centre, always accessible and dominated (*bestimmt*) by the shops and sites of city life.

County Library, Karlsruhe, model, interior

Museum in the University Complex, Marburg
1987

Interior with Sculpture by Georg Kolbe

This small museum in Marburg, more or less a pavilion in the garden of the university complex, was conceived as a *hortus conclusus* or small monastery cloister. The profile of the zinc roofs forges a link between the building and the obvious dominating image of the history of Marburg.

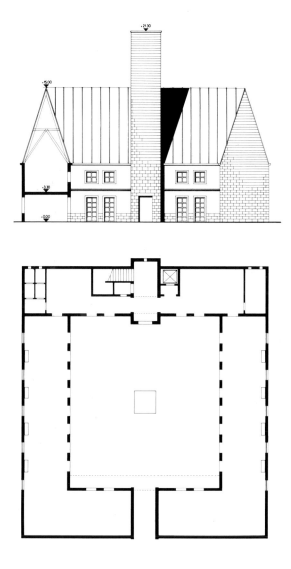

Museum, Marburg

193

Residential House, Southern Friedrichstadt, Berlin
1981 (construction until 1988)

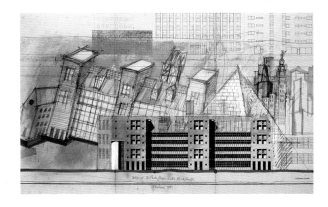

The large house in the Kochstrasse is today part of the new, as well as of the old, unity of Berlin. The corner column indicates the old border and the building measures itself against bourgeois Berlin architecture. It is easily recognisable in its urban environment and has become exemplary for modern residential building.

Southern Friedrichstadt, Berlin

Southern Friedrichstadt, Berlin

Southern Friedrichstadt, Berlin

197

Residential House in Rauchstrasse, Berlin
1983 (construction until 1985)

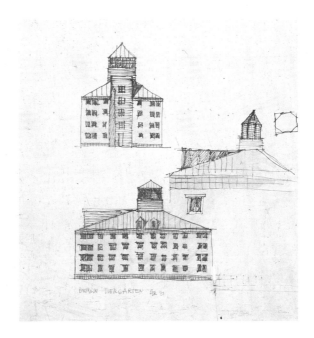

This building can be found in Rauchstrasse with one side facing a green space. In this case, I once again followed the example of Berlin architecture, above all with the yellow and red brick bands that alternate with one another (complementary to the roofs).

Rauchstrasse, Berlin

Rauchstrasse, Berlin

Rauchstrasse, Berlin

Museum of German History, Berlin
1988

The importance of this project was linked to the idea of Berlin as a capital city, taking into account its possible development, its technical capabilities and the reality of a building that will be constructed. I am convinced that one cannot judge it with instruments of criticism that fail to see the city as a capital.

I therefore believe that this Berlin museum could become a 'cathedral', returning to this term that I regard highly. Cathedrals, churches, museums, town halls and courts are places for the upkeep of the collective unconscious. The museum is the place of collective memories *par excellence*.

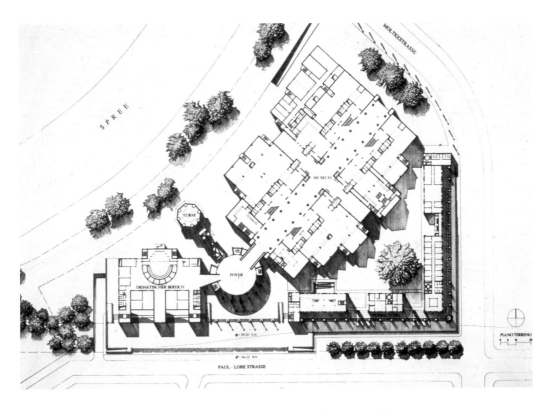

Museum of German History, Berlin, ground floor
and site plan (and *overleaf*)

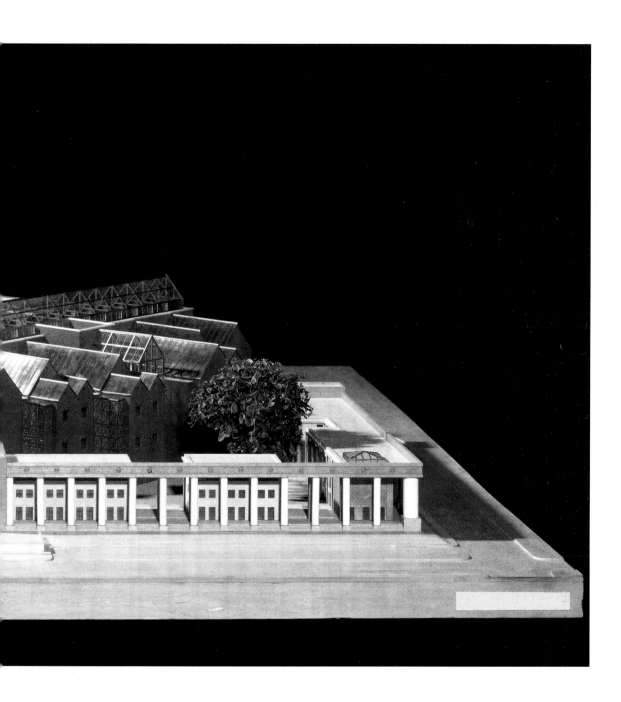

Potsdamer Platz, Berlin
1990

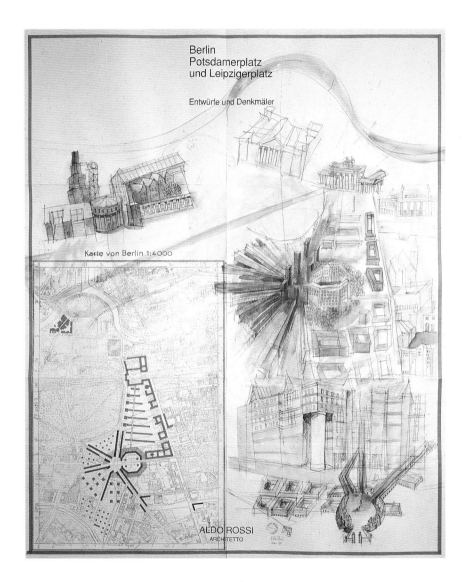

Friedrichstrasse, Berlin
1991

Landsberger Allee, Berlin
1991/92

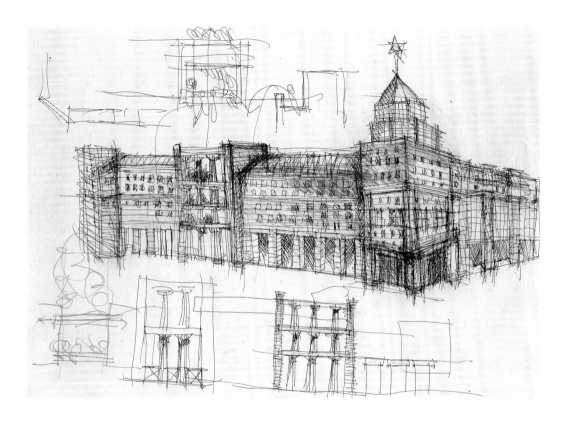

This building reflects two typologically typical aspects of Berlin architecture – the en-bloc building along a street linked to the standard height for eaves and the large, green inner space (the 'Berlin Hof' or courtyard) that was exemplary for the whole modern development of the city.

Landsberger Allee, Berlin (and *overleaf*)

PROJEKT AN DER LANDSBERGER ALLEE

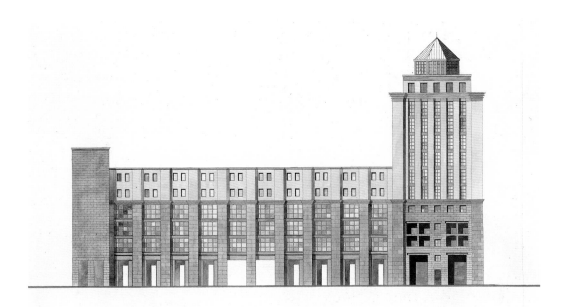

213

Schützenstrasse, Berlin
1991/92

This design is particularly interesting with regard to two aspects of the reconstruction of Berlin: first, the reconstruction and restoration of historical buildings, typical for the urban construction of the past; second, the construction of completely new buildings related to these.

Schützenstrasse, Berlin (and *overleaf*)

215

Segrate, Town Hall Public Space and Monument for the Partisans, 1965, project, p82

Milan, Housing Block in the Gallaratese Area 2, 1969-73, completed, p84

Modena, San Cataldo Cemetery (with G Braghieri), 1971, completion up until 1978, partially still under construction, p88

Fagnano Olona, Primary School, 1972-76, completed, p94

La Città Analoga (the Analogous City), 1977, p98

Broni, Secondary School, 1979, completed, p100

Venice, Teatro del Mondo, 1979, completed, p104

Giussano, Molteni Burial Chapel (with C Stead), 1980, completed, p108

Perugia, New Centre for the City Area Fontivegge (with G Braghieri, G Geronzi, M Scheurer), 1982-88, completed, p112

Borgoricco, New Town Hall (with M Scheurer, M Zancanella), 1983-88, completed, p116

Genoa, Reconstruction of the Carlo Felice Theatre (I Gardella, A Rossi with F Reinhart, A Sibilla), 1983-90, completed, p120

Turin, Office Building Casa Aurora (with G Braghieri, C Ciocca, F Marchesotti, M Scheurer, I Uva), 1984-87 completed, p124

Parma, Centro Torri (with G Braghieri, M Baracco, P Digiuni, M. Scheurer), 1985-88, completed, p128

Milan, Residential Building in the Vialba Area (with G Braghieri, G Ciocca, B Huet), 1985, completed, p132

Paris, Residential and Business Building in the La Villette-Sud Area (with C Zuber, B Huet), 1986, completed, p136

Fukuoka, Japan, Il Palazzo Hotel (with M Adjmi, T Horiguchi, S Uchida), 1987-89, completed, p140

Pennsylvania, Mount Pocon, USA, Single-Family House 1988-89 (with M Adjmi), completed, p144

Vassivière, France, Museum for Contemporary Art (with S Fera, C Fabre), 1988, completed, p146

Toronto, Canada, Lighthouse-Theatre (with M Adjmi), 1987, completed, p150

Milan, Construction of the Croce Rossa Square with the Pertini Monument, (with FS Fera, M Adjmi), 1988, completed, p152

Milan, Sports Palace (with B Agostino, G Da Pozzo, L Imberti, F Gatti), 1988, project, p156

Milan, Reconstruction and Extension of the Hotel Duca (with G Da Pozzo, M Scheurer), 1988, completed, p158

Zandaam, Holland, Tower with Sculpture Museum (with U Barbieri), 1989-90, completed, p162

Verbania, Lake Maggiore, Casa Alessi (with G Da Pozzo, L Imberti, F Gatti), 1989, project, p164

Castellanza, Cesare Cattaneo University Building (with A Balzani, M Brandolisio, F Gatti, L Imberti), 1990, p166

Maastricht, Netherlands, Bonnefanten Museum (with U Barbieri, G Da Pozzo, K Fatt Ho, M Kocher), 1990, under construction, p170

Milan, Church of San Carlo alla Barona in the Cascina Biance Area (with G Da Pozzo, SF Fera), 1990, project, p174

Seregno, Library, 1990, p176

List of Illustrations

Invisible Distances

Aldo Rossi

One day in May, Werther visits his place of birth on his way to the ducal hunting-lodge. Approaching the town, he greets all the old, familiar houses and their gardens. The new buildings, however, 'were hideous, as were all the other changes that had been made,' he wrote.[1] Even when confronted by the old house, in which he had lived, he remembers only 'the restlessness, the tears, the heaviness of heart, the deadly fear that I had to put up with in that hole.' He then goes down to the river. Looking at his surroundings becomes a problem of perception. He remembers how often he used to stand, looking at the flowing water until he was 'completely lost to himself, contemplating the invisible distances.'

The idea of this 'invisible distance' recalls the natural wisdom of antique writers and the equivocality of perception: 'What is the use of repeating the schoolboy words that it (the earth, footnote in the translation) is round? Man needs only a few clods of earth in order to enjoy himself on its surface, even less to find rest under it.' It is strange that Werther starts to speak twice about whether life is pointless, with the clarity and purposefulness of the suicidal man, each time referring to his surroundings and therefore to architecture, in a certain sense. The first time, his former house, described so bitterly as a 'hole', dissolves into memories of his youth, as if architecture were but a means of revealing the self. The second time, the earth has been reduced to a few clods of earth, good for only two things: love and death. This becomes clear from the beginning, where Werther came to the conclusion that he finds the changes made to the town hideous.

The feeling that he is overcome by – that of love – appears to annihilate Werther. At the same time, this feeling is also the reason that he regards above all the room he is in, as well as the perception of this room, as a sensory illusion (what is the use of the earth being round, one needs but a few clods of earth for love, even fewer for death, etc).

It almost appears as if the world were but an attempt to forget the things we can never possess.

There are few visions – not even Adolf Loos' famous dictum that architecture can be equated with a funerary monument[2] – that allow the world and its buildings to shrink to such uselessness. Architecture is reduced to little more than decoration. One knows that this is untrue. Yet these 'few clods of earth' can be equated with a reduction of architecture that I have always liked. This also reinforces my deep, perhaps exaggerated, distaste for all theories that portray the architect as artist and bringer of comfort, as can be found in texts concerning modern architecture.

Although one can deny that architecture can bring any form of comfort, it still exists and therefore has a history and a process of evolution, even if this plays but a small part in our lives. A short while ago, I visited the large shrine of Ise in Japan, and many of my earlier ideas on architecture came to mind. Two identical, ancient temples stand next to each other on this almost untouched spot. They are, however, only ancient in so far as one of both temples is always constructed anew. The older temple is destroyed every twenty-five years, as soon as its neighbour has been completed. The new one always has only one piece of wood from the older temple. I do not think there are many examples of a similar repetition of the process of building, encompassing the idea of building and which also demonstrate such indifference towards architecture.

When people grow older, so do their memories. This could be a truism or also a revelation. In any case, I believe it to be correct and connect this experience with the way one perceives things. That is to say, things are given a value by being perceived. 'Perceiving' things does not, however, mean that one has 'seen them', in this case. Perceiving the meaning of the shrine of Ise seems to me to be in this vein. It is not the material that is important, whether it be old or new, neither is the object itself. It is only the idea that counts, expressed by the activity, repeated after having been recognised on the first occasion. One no longer needs to question its meaning. In Western culture, the equivalent of this could, to a certain extent, be ritual. This has, however, little to do with the idea of the fragmentary. Perhaps this is also because the fragment does not demand an all-inclusive image, strong enough to liberate itself from its own materiality. I am thinking of Classicism, of the 'white stones' of the culture of Humanism and of the cult of the fragmentary. Therefore, this phenomenon of repetition, which is always new, disturbs our equanimity, pushes us beyond the norm, beyond the usual framework of things, in the literal sense of the word, even if this is by nature something unified. There is undoubtedly a unity in these matters and one must find their core. It seems to me sometimes that this core is equal to growth. I shall explain why I use this term, at the same time realising that I understand it as both a limit and as a necessity. It is as if we should start noticing that a child is not growing. This would make us unhappy, while at the same time we have already realised that its childhood is over as soon as it has stopped growing. I speak of growing, or growth, as I believe that I am now able to understand a passage in the eighth book of Quintilian's 'Institutio oratoria' – strangely enough, in relation to architecture. It puzzled me for a great length of time, although it had always impressed me as a strange manner. In the passage, Quintilian speaks of a technique of growth. He adds that something could grow so large, with the aid of this technique, that it could then not possibly grow any larger (*Nam est hoc agendi genus et tantum aliquid efficere, ut non possit augeri*).

This technique of growth is exactly the borderline that the artist reaches, with a kind of terror, for which there is no explanation. Boullée's writings, Pontormo's diary and many other texts, where artists speak about themselves, testify to this.

Perhaps this idea of growth belongs to the realm of pure technique – as if one could possess a tool with which one could measure it.

Or perhaps it is the secret, found in unfinished buildings, which we love because their growth seems to result from a catastrophe, a displacement or giving something up (as is actually often the case) and is not based on a rational decision.

When I write about architecture, I believe that I can explain all these problems in a general manner, while not knowing how much it has to do with my own architecture. Today, it seems that this something – which is perhaps nothing at all – that always lies between the thought and its articulation, between the past and future, is disappearing increasingly. Therefore, when I wrote that 'it is strange how similar I am to myself', it is perhaps because I did not know how to grasp this something, that defines differences, or the difference between the things that we create.

The projects progress and are still similar to one another. By working in various places with a variety of people, we must increasingly stand outside ourselves in order to hear the sonority of the world. By hearing this, we are able to remain ourselves. Therefore, the interest we take in what we call art, architecture or even technology increases both in ourselves and others.

Often, however, the sonority of the world leads us back to the relativity of the child or of the family. My last project, or rather the one that is being constructed at the moment in Japan (1989), is, to a certain extent, the repetition of a project on Lake Como, the sports hall in Olginate. It is as if a building on that lake had foreseen the Far East (even if the Lombard lake does not actually appertain to any geographical or national reality) and as if Fukuoka had already existed as a possibility in my architecture.

Leaving our shell in order to hear the sonority of the world, or also that of our century – one of Walter Benjamin's most beautiful images[3] – this is an essential quality of my most recent projects. Therefore, it does not bother me if my buildings are to be found in Texas, Japan or Berlin, or, as in the case of the beautiful museum at Vassivière, on a distant isle in the heart of the Limousin, one of the least known areas of France.

I do not want to speak of my buildings at this point. I would much rather return to the method of minute description, without focusing on individual designs. Only a new 'école du regard' can spare us needless details and make us aware of the actual significance of the constructions.

Where this lies, I do not know.

Perhaps only in those few clods of earth, in forgetting architecture and the whole of technology. It would increasingly come close to an attempt at forgetting all that we cannot possess.

Today, I think that the town that Werther rediscovered, where the house became a hole filled with restlessness, tears and deadly fear, is no longer simply a sad, poetic image, but has become a real place in our everyday lives.

Our cities depress me. It seems that all of us that have some connection to building (engineers, architects, surveyors, masons etc) are more or less scientific instruments in the interventions in their structure. These interventions are moreover useless.

I recall an article that was written somewhere, on some occasion that I have forgotten, with the title: *What Should we do with Architecture?*

The answer does not seem to me to be hugely difficult. If one liberates oneself from all rhetorical and demagogic clutter, one sees architecture as a type of art (or as a craft). It is enough to do a thing well. This is a question of ethics and of work experience.

On the impulse of a mood or memory, I began with the young Werther and the clarity of mind that a suicidal man is in possession of. I also wish to end this reflection with his words: he comes to the prince elector's hunting lodge (of which he tells us nothing) and after a few remarks about people encountered there, remarks on the prince elector himself: 'Even he praises my intellect and talents more than this heart, that is my sole pride, the sole source of everything, of all strength, bliss and all misery.'

Art, including architecture and even science, is perhaps a part of all these phenomena.

The architecture of the past, the present and, above all, of the future is an invisible distance for us. The future is not the noise of trams in an old-fashioned Milan, which certain Futurists claimed as being progressive. Simpletons always regard things from a greater degree of proximity and they end up solving yesterday's problems.

The hero I have quoted wishes to say that invisible distances express passion, pulling the logic of the everyday with it. To know that the earth is round is not sufficient for us to be moved, either in an intellectual or a personal manner.

To try to change the world is possible, even if this is only in fragments, thereby forgetting what we cannot possess.

Notes

1 Rossi quotes from the Italian translation of the second edition (1783-86) of *The Sorrows of Young Werther* in: Johann Wolfgang Goethe, Gedenkausgabe, vol 4, edited by Ernst Beutler, Zurich, 1953, pp 454-55.
2 'Only a tiny part of architecture has artistic value: the grave and the monument. Everything else, serving its purpose, should be excluded from the realm of art.' in: Adolf Loos, Trotzdem, second larger edition, Innsbruck, 1931, p 107.
3 Compare to Walter Benjamin, *Berliner Kindheit*, Frankfurt a. M. 1950, p 74: 'I lived like a mollusc in its shell – the nineteenth century that now lies before me, hollow like an empty shell.'

Aldo Rossi's essay 'Invisible Distances' first appeared in *Architettura in Italia Oggi*, Rome 1989, entitled 'Le distanze invisibile'. Taken from the book *Aldo Rossi, Buildings and Projects, 1981-91*.

© German edition, Artemis Verlag, Zürich, 1991.

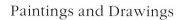

Paintings and Drawings

Fragment, 1979

Fragment, 1987

Venetian interior, 1981

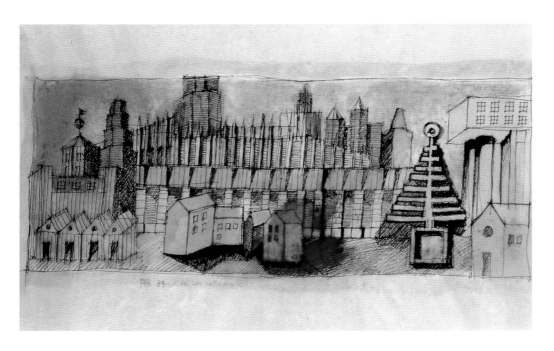

City with Cathedral, 1984

San Carlone, 1990

Study of Borgoricco, 1986

231

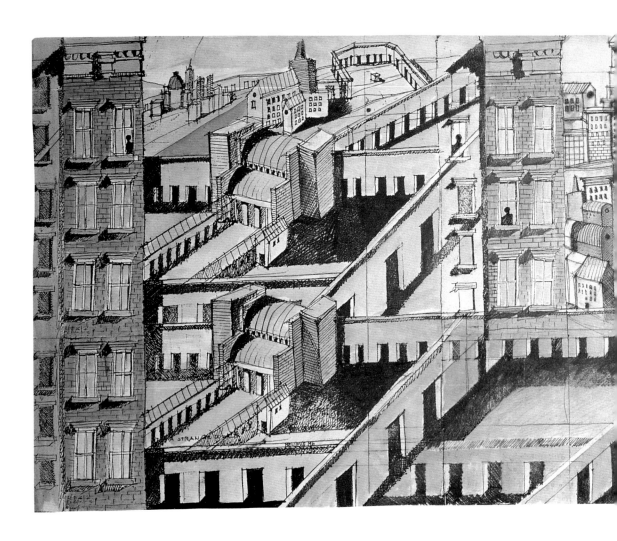

Study of Maastricht, 1990

234

Biography

1931 Born 3rd May in Milan.
Lived in a house on Lake Como during the war.
Attended the monastic Somasca School and later the archepiscopal Allesandro Volta High School in Lecco.

1949 Commenced study at Milan Polytechnic.

1955 A number of travels led Rossi to Rome and abroad, above all to the Soviet Union.
Asked by Ernesto N Rogers to work for *Casabella Continuità* where he remained an editor until the magazine was discontinued in 1964.

1956 Commenced work for Ignazio Gardella and Marco Zanuso.

1959 Received diploma from Milan Polytechnic.

1963 Became Ludovico Quaroni's assistant at the School for Urban Planning, Arezzo.
Also Carlo Aymonino's assistant in the Architectural Institute.
at the University of Venice.

1965 Taught at Milan Polytechnic.
Travel to Spain and works with Salvatore Tarrago.

1966 Publication of his book *L'Architettura della Città*.

1970 Won competition for the chair of historical building in Palermo.

1971 Due to politico-cultural activities at the university, Rossi was banned from teaching in Italy for four years.

1972 Taught at the confederate polytechnic college in Zurich. Began to work with Gianni Braghieri.

1973 Director of the international architectural section at the Milan Triennale.
Completes his film *Ornamento e Delitto*.

1975 After being permitted to teach again, Rossi was asked to teach architectural composition at the University of Venice.

1976 Taught in the USA (Cornell University, Ithaca and Cooper Union, New York).
Lectured in Buenos Aires.
Worked at the Institute for Architecture and Urban Studies in New York.

1979 Member of the Academy of San Luca.

1980 Guest professor at Yale University.

1984 First prize in the competition for the Carlo Felice Theatre in Genoa.

1986 The exhibition 'Architectural Designs' shown at the Albertina Gallery in Turin.
Exhibition in Madrid.
The exhibition 'Hendrik Petrus Berlage' shown at the Venice Biennale.
1987 First Italian architect to have an exhibition in Moscow.
First prize in international competition for La Villette-Sud in Paris.
1988 Joint exhibition in New York and London.
First prize in the international competition for the Museum of German History in Berlin.
1989 Walter Gropius conference in Harvard.
1990 Winner of the Pritzker Prize 1991.
1991 Winner of the AIA Honour Award 1991.
Prize for best architecture of the City of Fukuoka with 'Il Palazzo' Hotel.
Retrospective exhibition at the Centre Georges Pompidou in Paris.
Retrospective exhibition in the Berlage Stock Exchange in Amsterdam.
1992 Winner of the 1991 Thomas Jefferson Medal in Architecture.

END